Fodor's
Pocket
Jamaica

P9-BYM-046

Reprinted from *Fodor's Caribbean*

Fodor's Travel Publications, Inc.
New York • Toronto • London •
Sydney • Auckland

ISBN 0–679–02746–7

Fodor's Pocket Jamaica

Editor: Melanie A. Roth
Contributors: Robert Blake, Tracy Patruno,
Laurie Senz
Creative Director: Fabrizio La Rocca
Cartographer: David Lindroth
Illustrator: Karl Tanner
Cover Photograph: Peter Guttman
Design: Vignelli Associates

Special Sales

Fodor's Travel Publications are available at
special discounts for sales promotions or premi-
ums. Special editions, including personalized
covers, excerpts of existing guides, and corporate imprints, can be created in large quantities
for special needs. For more information, contact
your local bookseller or write to Special Markets, Fodor's Travel Publications, 201 E. 50th
St., New York, NY 10022; Random House of
Canada, Ltd., Marketing Dept. 1265 Aerowood
Dr., Mississauga, Ontario L4W 1B9; Fodor's
Travel Publications, 20 Vauxhall Bridge Rd.,
London, England SW1V 2SA.

Contents

Foreword

Fodor's Pocket Jamaica is intended especially for the new or short-term visitor who wants a complete but concise account of the most exciting places to see and the most interesting things to do.

Those who plan to spend more time in the Caribbean, or seek additional information about areas of interest, will want to consult *Fodor's Caribbean* for in-depth coverage of the area.

While every care has been taken to assure the accuracy of the information in this guide, the passage of time will always bring change, and consequently, the publisher cannot accept responsibility for errors that may occur.

All prices and opening times quoted here are based on information supplied to us at press time. Hours and admission fees may change, however, and the prudent traveler will avoid inconvenience by calling ahead.

Fodor's wants to hear about your travel experiences, both pleasant and unpleasant. When a hotel or restaurant fails to live up to its billing, let us know and we will investigate the complaint and revise our entries where the facts warrant it.

Send your letters to the editors of Fodor's Travel Publications, 201 East 50th Street, New York, NY 10022.

Jamaica

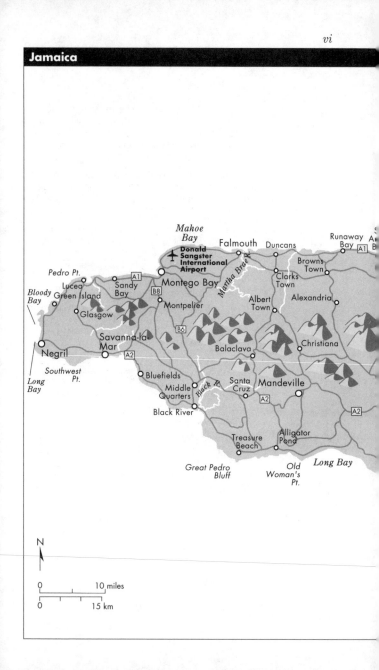

Mahoe Bay

Falmouth   Duncans   Runaway Bay   A1 B

Donald Sangster International Airport

Pedro Pt.

Bloody Bay   Lucea   Green Island

Sandy Bay   A1

Montego Bay   B8

Browns Town

Clarks Town   Albert Town   Alexandria

Glasgow   Montpelier   B6

Savanna-la-Mar   A2

Balaclava   Christiana

Negril

Southwest Pt.

Long Bay

Bluefields

Middle Quarters   Black R.   Santa Cruz   Mandeville

Black River   A2   A2

Treasure Beach   Alligator Pond

Great Pedro Bluff   Old Woman's Pt.   Long Bay

N

0   10 miles

0   15 km

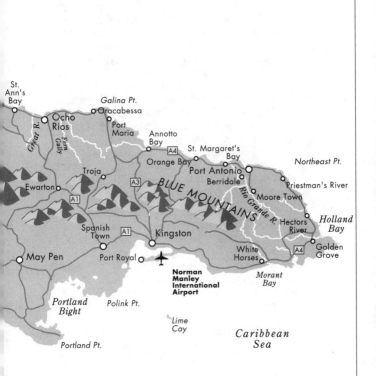

Introduction

Updated by Laurie S. Senz

The third-largest island in the Caribbean (after Cuba and Puerto Rico), the English-speaking nation of Jamaica enjoys a considerable self-sufficiency based on tourism, agriculture, and mining. Its physical attractions include jungle mountaintops, clear waterfalls, and unforgettable beaches, yet the country's greatest resource may be the Jamaicans themselves. Although 95% of the population trace their bloodlines to Africa, their national origins lie in Great Britain, the Middle East, India, China, Germany, Portugal, South America, and many of the other islands in the Caribbean. Their cultural life is a wealthy one; the music, art, and cuisine of Jamaica are vibrant, with a spirit easy to sense but as hard to describe as the rhythms of reggae or a flourish of the streetwise patois.

Jamaica is unusual in that in addition to such pleasure capitals of the north coast as Montego Bay and Ocho Rios, it has a real capital in Kingston. For all its congestion and for all the disparity between city life and the bikinis and parasails to the north, Kingston is the true heart and head of the island. This is the place where politics, literature, music, and art wrestle for acceptance in the largest English-speaking city south of Miami, its actual population of nearly 1 million bolstered by the emotional membership of virtually all Jamaicans.

The first people known to have reached Jamaica were the Arawaks, Indians who paddled their canoes from the Orinoco region of South America about a thousand years after the death of Christ. Then, in 1494, Christopher Columbus stepped ashore at what is now called Discovery Bay. Having spent four centuries on the island, the Arawaks had little notion that his feet on their sand would mean their extinction within 50 years.

What is now St. Ann's Bay was established as New Seville in 1509 and served as the Spanish capital until the local government crossed the island to Santiago de la Vega (now Spanish Town). The Spaniards were never impressed with Jamaica; their searches found no precious metals, and they let the island fester in poverty for 161 years. When 5,000 British soldiers and sailors appeared in Kingston Harbor in 1655, the Spaniards did not put up a fight.

The arrival of the English, and the three centuries of rule that followed, provided Jamaica with the surprisingly genteel underpinnings of its present life—and the rousing pirate tradition fueled by rum that enlivened a long period of Caribbean history. The British buccaneer Henry Morgan counted Jamaica's governor as one of his closest friends and enjoyed the protection of His Majesty's government no matter what he chose to plunder. Port Royal, once said to be the "wickedest city of Christendom," grew up on a spit of land across from present-day Kingston precisely because it served so many interests. Morgan and his brigands were delighted to have such a haven, and the people of Jamaica profited by being able to buy pirate booty there at terrific bargains.

Morgan enjoyed a prosperous life; he was knighted and made lieutenant governor of Jamaica before the age of 30, and, like every good bureaucrat, he died in bed and was given a state funeral. Port Royal fared less well. On June 7, 1692, an earthquake tilted two-thirds of the city into the sea, the tidal wave that followed the last tremors washed away millions in pirate treasure, and Port Royal simply disappeared. In recent years divers have turned up some of the treasure, but most of it still lies in the depths, adding an exotic quality to the water sports pursued along Kingston's reefs.

The very British 18th century was a time of prosperity in Jamaica. This was the age of the sugar baron, who ruled his plantation great house and made the island the largest sugar-producing colony in the world. Because sugar fortunes were built on slave labor, however, production became less profitable when the Jamaican slave trade was abolished in 1807 and slavery was ended in 1838.

As was often the case in colonies, a national identity came to supplant allegiance to the British in the hearts and minds of Jamaicans. This new identity was given official recognition on August 6, 1962, when Jamaica became an independent nation with loose ties to the Commonwealth. The island today has a democratic form of government led by a prime minister and a cabinet of fellow ministers.

1 Essential Information

Before You Go

Tourist Information

Contact the **Jamaica Tourist Board,** 801 2nd Ave., 20th Floor, New York, NY 10017, tel. 212/856–9727, 800/233–4JTB; fax 212/856–9730; 500 North Michigan Ave., Suite 1030, Chicago, IL 60611, tel. 312/527–1296, fax 312/527–1472; 1320 S. Dixie Hwy., Coral Gables, FL 33146, tel. 305/665–0557, fax 305/666–7239; 8214 Westchester, Suite 500, Dallas, TX 75225, tel. 214/361–8778, fax 214/361–7049; 3440 Wilshire Blvd., Suite 1207, Los Angeles, CA 90010, tel. 213/384–1123, fax 213/384–1123. **In Canada:** 1 Eglinton Ave. E, Suite 616, Toronto, Ontario M4P 3A1, tel. 416/482–7850, fax 416/482–1730. **In the United Kingdom:** 1–2 Prince Consort Rd., London, SW7 2BZ, tel. 071/224–0505, fax 071/224–0551.

What to Pack

Pack light because baggage carts are scarce at airports and luggage restrictions are tight.

Clothing Dress in Jamaica is light and casual. Bring loose-fitting clothes made of natural fabrics to see you through days of heat and high humidity. Take a cover-up for the beaches, not only to protect you from the sun, but also to wear to and from your hotel room. A sun hat is advisable, but you don't have to pack one, since inexpensive straw hats are available everywhere. For shopping and sightseeing, bring walking shorts, jeans, T-shirts, long-sleeve cotton shirts, slacks, and sundresses. You'll need a sweater in the many glacially air-conditioned hotels and restaurants, for protection from the trade winds, and at higher altitudes. Evenings are casual, but "casual" can range from really informal to casually elegant, depending on the establishment. A tie is rarely required but jackets are sometimes required in the fancier restaurants and casinos.

Adapters, Converters, Transformers The general rule in the Caribbean is 110 and 120 volts AC, and the outlets take the same two-prong plugs found in the United States, but there are a number of exceptions, particularly on the French islands and on some islands with a British heritage. To be sure, check with your hotel when making reservations.

You may need an adapter plug, plus a converter, which reduces the voltage entering the appliance from 220 to 110 volts. There are converters for high-wattage appliances (such as hair dryers), low-wattage items (such as electric toothbrushes and razors), and combination models. Hotels sometimes have outlets marked "For Shavers Only" near the sink; these are 110-volt outlets for low-wattage appliances; don't use them for a high-wattage appliance.

Miscellaneous Bring a spare pair of eyeglasses, sunglasses, or contact lenses, and if you have a health problem that may require you to purchase a prescription drug, have your doctor write a prescription using its generic name, since nomenclature varies from island to island. Better still, take enough to last the duration of the trip: Although you can probably find what you need in the pharmacies, you may need a local doctor's prescription. You'll want an umbrella during the rainy season; leave the plastic or nylon raincoats at home, since they're extremely uncomfortable in hot, humid weather. Bring suntan lotion and film from home; they're much more expensive on the islands. You'll need insect repellent, too, especially if you plan to walk through rain forests or visit during the rainy season.

Luggage Free airline baggage allowances depend on the
Regulations airline, the route, and the class of your ticket; ask in advance. In general, on domestic flights and on international flights between the United States and foreign destinations, you are entitled to check two bags—neither exceeding 62 inches, or 158 centimeters (length + width + height), or weighing more than 70 pounds (32 kilograms). A third piece may be brought aboard as a carry-on; its total dimensions are generally limited to less than 45 inches (114 centimeters) so it will fit easily under the seat in front of you or in the overhead compartment. In the United States, the Federal Aviation Administration (FAA) gives airlines broad latitude to limit carry-on allowances and tailor them to different aircraft

and operational conditions. Charges for excess, oversize, or overweight pieces vary.

Safeguarding Your Luggage Before leaving home, itemize the contents of your bags and their worth in case they go astray. To minimize that risk, tag them inside and out with your name, address, and phone number. (If you use your home address, cover it so that potential thieves can't see it.) If your bags do not arrive with you, or if you detect damage, file a written report with the airline immediately— before you leave the airport.

Getting Money from Home

Cash Machines Many automated-teller machines (ATMs) are tied to international networks such as **Cirrus** and **Plus,** both of which have expanded their service in the Caribbean. You can use your bank card at ATMs away from home to withdraw money from an account and get cash advances on a credit-card account if your card has been programmed with a personal identification number, or PIN. Check in advance on limits on withdrawals and cash advances within specified periods. Ask whether your bank-card or credit-card PIN number will need to be reprogrammed for use in the area you'll be visiting. Four digits are commonly used overseas. Note that Discover is accepted only in the United States. On cash advances you are charged interest from the day you receive the money from ATMs as well as from tellers. Although transaction fees for ATM withdrawals abroad may be higher than fees for withdrawals at home, Cirrus and Plus exchange rates tend to be good. Be sure to plan ahead: Obtain ATM locations and the names of affiliated cash-machine networks before departure. For specific foreign Cirrus locations, call 800/424–7787; for foreign Plus locations, consult the Plus directory at your local bank.

Wiring Money You don't have to be a cardholder to send or receive a **MoneyGram from American Express** for up to $10,000. Go to a MoneyGram agent in retail and convenience stores and American Express travel offices, pay up to $1,000 with a credit card and anything over that in cash. You are allowed a free long-distance call to give the transaction code to your intended recipient, who needs only present identification and the reference number to the nearest MoneyGram agent to pick up the cash. MoneyGram agents are in more than 70 countries (call 800/926–9400 for locations). Fees range from 3% to 10%, depending on the amount and how you pay.

You can also use **Western Union.** To wire money, take either cash or a check to the nearest office or call and use your MasterCard or Visa. Money sent from the United States or Canada will be available for pickup at agent locations in the Caribbean within minutes. Once the money is in the system it can be picked up at *any* one of 22,000 locations (call 800/325–6000 for the one nearest you).

Traveling with Cameras, Camcorders, and Laptops

Film and Cameras If your camera is new or if you haven't used it for a while, shoot and develop a few rolls of film before leaving home. Store film in a cool, dry place—never in the car's glove compartment or on the shelf under the rear window.

Airport security X-rays generally aren't harmful to film with ISO below 400. To protect your film, carry it with you in a clear plastic bag and ask for a hand inspection. Such requests are honored at U.S. airports, up to the inspector abroad. Don't depend on a lead-lined bag to protect film in checked luggage—the airline may increase the radiation to see what's inside. Call the Kodak Information Center (tel. 800/242–2424) for details.

Camcorders Before your trip, put camcorders through their paces, invest in a skylight filter to protect the lens, and check all the batteries. Most newer camcorders are equipped with a universal or worldwide AC adapter charger (or multivoltage converter) usable whether the voltage is 110 or 220. All that's needed is the appropriate plug.

Videotape Videotape is not damaged by X-rays, but it may be harmed by the magnetic field of a walk-through metal detector, so ask for a hand-check. Airport security personnel may want you to turn on the camcorder to prove that it's what it appears to be, so make sure the battery is charged.

Laptops Security X-rays do not harm hard-disk or floppy-disk storage, but you may request a hand-check, at which point you may be asked to turn on the computer to prove that it is what it appears to be. (Check your battery before departure.) Most airlines allow you to use your laptop aloft except during takeoff and landing (so as not to interfere with navigation equipment). For international travel, register your foreign-made laptop with U.S. Customs as you leave the country. If your laptop is U.S.-made, call the Jamaican consulate to find out whether it should be registered with customs upon arrival. Before departure, find out about repair facilities on the island, and don't forget any transformer or adapter plug you may need.

Staying Healthy

Few real hazards threaten the health of a visitor to Jamaica. The small lizards that seem to have overrun the island are harmless, and poisonous snakes are hard to find. The worst problem may well be a tiny sand fly known as the "no-see-um," which tends to appear after a rain, near wet or swampy ground, and around sunset. If you feel particularly vulnerable to insect bites, bring along a good repellent.

Sunburn or sunstroke can also be serious problems. Even people who are not normally bothered by strong sun should head here with a long-sleeve shirt, a hat, and long pants or a beach wrap. These are essential for a day on a boat but are also advisable for midday at the beach and whenever you go out sightseeing. Also carry some sunblock lotion for nose, ears, and other sensitive areas such as eyelids, ankles, etc. Limit your sun time for the first few days until you become used to the heat. And be sure to drink enough liquids.

Scuba divers take note: PADI (the Professional Association of Diving Instructors) recommends that you not scuba dive and fly within a 24-hour period.

Finding a Doctor   The **International Association for Medical Assistance to Travelers** (IAMAT, 417 Center St., Lewiston, NY 14092, tel. 716/754–4883; 40 Regal Rd., Guelph, Ontario N1K 1B5; 57 Voirets, 1212 Grand-Lancy, Geneva Switzerland) publishes a worldwide directory of English-speaking physicians whose qualifications meet IAMAT standards and who have agreed to treat members for a set fee. Membership is free.

Assistance Companies   Pretrip medical referrals, emergency evacuation or repatriation, 24-hour telephone hot lines for medical consultation, dispatch of medical personnel, relay of medical records, up-front cash for emergencies, and other personal and legal assistance are among the services provided by several membership organizations specializing in medical assistance to travelers. Among them are **International SOS Assistance** (Box 11568, Philadelphia, PA 19116, tel. 215/244–1500 or 800/523–8930; Box 466, Pl. Bonaventure, Montréal, Québec, H5A 1C1, tel. 514/874–7674 or 800/363–0263), **Medex Assistance Corporation** (Box 10623, Baltimore, MD 21285, tel. 410/296–2530 or 800/874–9125), **Near Services** (450 Prairie Ave., Suite 101, Calumet City, IL 60409, tel. 708/868–6700 or 800/654–6700), and **Travel Assistance International** (1133 15th St. NW, Suite 400, Washington, DC 20005, tel. 202/331–1609 or 800/821–2828). Because these companies will also sell you death-and-dismemberment, trip-cancellation, and other insurance coverage, there is some overlap with the travel-insurance policies discussed under Insurance, *below.*

Publications   *The Safe Travel Book* by Peter Savage ($12.95; Lexington Books, 866 3rd Ave., New York, NY 10022, tel. 212/702–4771 or 800/257–5755, fax 800/562–1272) is packed with handy lists and phone numbers to make your trip smooth. *Traveler's Medical Resource* by William W. Forgey ($19.95; ICS Books, Inc., 1 Tower Plaza, 107 E. 89th Ave., Merrillville, IN 45410, tel. 800/541–7323) is also a good, authoritative guide to care overseas.

Insurance

Most tour operators, travel agents, and insurance agents sell specialized health-and-accident, flight, trip-cancellation, and luggage insurance as well as comprehensive policies with some or all of these features. But before you make any purchase, review your existing health and home-owner policies to find out whether they cover expenses incurred while traveling.

Health-and-Accident Insurance Specific policy provisions of supplemental health-and-accident insurance for travelers include reimbursement for from $1,000 to $150,000 worth of medical and/or dental expenses caused by an accident or illness during a trip. The personal-accident or death-and-dismemberment provision pays a lump sum to your beneficiaries if you die or to you if you lose a limb or your eyesight; the lump sum awarded can range from $15,000 to $500,000. The medical-assistance provision may reimburse you for the cost of referrals, evacuation, or repatriation and other services, or it may automatically enroll you as a member of a particular medical-assistance company (*see* Assistance Companies, *above*).

Flight Insurance Often bought as a last-minute impulse at the airport, flight insurance pays a lump sum when a plane crashes either to a beneficiary if the insured dies or sometimes to a surviving passenger who loses eyesight or a limb. Like most impulse buys, flight insurance is expensive and basically unnecessary. It supplements the airlines' coverage described in the limits-of-liability paragraphs on your ticket. Charging an airline ticket to a major credit card often automatically entitles you to coverage and may also embrace travel by bus, train, and ship.

Baggage Insurance In the event of loss, damage, or theft on international flights, airlines' liability is $20 per kilogram for checked baggage (roughly about $640 per 70-pound bag) and $400 per passenger for unchecked baggage. On domestic flights, the ceiling is $1,250 per passenger. Excess-valuation insurance can be bought directly from the airline at check-in for about $10 per $1,000 worth of coverage. However, you cannot buy it at any price for the rather extensive list of excluded items shown on your airline ticket.

Trip Insurance

Trip-cancellation-and-interruption insurance protects you in the event you are unable to undertake or finish your trip, especially if your airline ticket, cruise, or package tour does not allow changes or cancellations. The amount of coverage you purchase should equal the cost of your trip should you, a traveling companion, or a family member fall ill, forcing you to stay home, plus the nondiscounted one-way airline ticket you would need to buy if you had to return home early. Read the fine print carefully, especially sections defining "family member" and "preexisting medical conditions." **Default** or **bankruptcy insurance** protects you against a supplier's failure to deliver. Such policies often do not cover default by a travel agency, tour operator, airline, or cruise line if you bought your tour and the coverage directly from the firm in question. Tours packaged by one of the 33 members of the United States Tour Operators Association (USTOA, 211 E. 51st St., Suite 12B, New York, NY 10022, tel. 212/750–7371), which requires members to maintain $1 million each in an account to reimburse clients in case of default, are likely to present the fewest difficulties. Even better, pay for travel arrangements with a major credit card, so that you can refuse to pay the bill if services have not been rendered—and let the card company fight your battles.

Comprehensive Policies

Companies supplying comprehensive policies with some or all of the above features include **Access America, Inc.** (Box 90315, Richmond, VA 23230, tel. 800/284–8300); **Carefree Travel Insurance** (Box 310, 120 Mineola Blvd., Mineola, NY 11501, tel. 516/294–0220 or 800/323–3149); **Tele-Trip** (Mutual of Omaha Plaza, Box 31762, Omaha, NE 68131, tel. 800/228–9792); **The Travelers Companies** (1 Tower Sq., Hartford, CT 06183, tel. 203/277–0111 or 800/243–3174); **Travel Guard International** (1145 Clark St., Stevens Point, WI 54481, tel. 715/345–0505 or 800/782–5151); and **Wallach and Company, Inc.** (107 W. Federal St., Box 480, Middleburg, VA 22117, tel. 703/687–3166 or 800/237–6615).

Student and Youth Travel

Travel Agencies   **Council Travel Services (CTS),** a subsidiary of the nonprofit Council on International Educational Exchange, specializes in low-cost travel arrangements abroad for students and is the exclusive U.S. agent for several discount cards. Also newly available from CTS are domestic air passes for bargain travel within the United States. CIEE's twice-yearly *Student Travels* magazine is available at the CTS office at CIEE headquarters (205 E. 42nd St., 16th Floor, New York, NY 10017, tel. 212/661–1450) and in Boston (tel. 617/266–1926), Miami (tel. 305/670–9261), Los Angeles (tel. 310/208–3551), and at 43 branches in college towns nationwide (free in person, $1 by mail). **Campus Connections** (1100 East Marlton Pike, Cherry Hill, NJ 08034, tel. 800/428–3235) specializes in discounted accommodations and airfares for students. The **Educational Travel Center** (438 N. Frances St., Madison, WI 53703, tel. 608/256–5551) offers low-cost domestic and international airline tickets, mostly for flights departing from Chicago, and rail passes. Other travel agencies catering to students include **TMI Student Travel** (1146 Pleasant St., Watertown, MA 02172, tel. 617/661–8187 or 800/245–3672) and **Travel Cuts** (187 College St., Toronto, Ontario M5T 1P7, tel. 416/979–2406).

Discount Cards   For discounts on transportation and on museum and attractions admissions, buy the **International Student Identity Card** (ISIC) if you're a bona fide student or the **International Youth Card** (IYC) if you're under 26. In the United States, the ISIC and IYC cards cost $15 each and include basic travel accident and sickness coverage. Apply to **CIEE** (*see* address *above*, tel. 212/661–1414; the application is in *Student Travels*). In Canada, the cards are available for $15 each from **Travel Cuts** (*see above*). In the United Kingdom, they cost £5 and £4, respectively, at student unions and student travel companies, including Council Travel's London office (28A Poland St., London W1V 3DB, tel. 071/437–7767).

Traveling with Children

Tour Operators
Grandtravel (6900 Wisconsin Ave., Suite 706, Chevy Chase, MD 20815, tel. 301/986–0790 or 800/247–7651) offers international and domestic tours for people traveling with their grandchildren. The catalogue, as charmingly written and illustrated as a children's book, positively invites armchair traveling with lap-sitters aboard. **Rascals in Paradise** (650 5th St., Suite 505, San Francisco, CA 94107, tel. 415/978–9800 or 800/872–7225) specializes in programs for families.

Publications
Newsletters
Family Travel Times, published 10 times a year by **Travel With Your Children** (TWYCH, 45 W. 18th St., 7th Floor Tower, New York, NY 10011, tel. 212/206–0688; annual subscription $55), covers destinations, types of vacations, and modes of travel. TWYCH also publishes *Cruising with Children.*

Books
Great Vacations with Your Kids, by Dorothy Jordon and Marjorie Cohen ($13; Penguin USA, 120 Woodbine St., Bergenfield, NJ 07621, tel. 800/253–6476), and *Traveling with Children— And Enjoying It,* by Arlene K. Butler ($11.95 plus $3 shipping; Globe Pequot Press, Box 833, 6 Business Park Rd., Old Saybrook, CT 06475, tel. 800/243–0495; in CT, 800/962–0973) help you plan your trip with children, from toddlers to teens. From the same publisher are *Recommended Family Resorts in the United States, Canada, and the Caribbean,* by Jane Wilford with Janet Tice ($12.95), and *Recommended Family Inns of America* ($12.95).

Getting There
Airfares
On international flights, the fare for infants under age 2 not occupying a seat is generally either free or 10% of the accompanying adult's fare; children ages 2 to 11 usually pay half to two-thirds of the adult fare. On domestic flights, children under 2 not occupying a seat travel free, and older children currently travel on the "lowest applicable" adult fare. Some routes in the Caribbean are considered neither international nor domestic and have still other rules; check with your airline.

Baggage
In general, infants paying 10% of the adult fare are allowed one carry-on bag, not to exceed 70

pounds or 45 inches (length + width + height) and a collapsible stroller; check with the airline before departure, because you may be allowed less if the flight is full. The adult baggage allowance applies to children paying half or more of the adult fare.

Safety Seats   The FAA recommends the use of safety seats aloft and details approved models in the free leaflet **"Child/Infant Safety Seats Recommended for Use in Aircraft"** (available from the Federal Aviation Administration, APA–200, 800 Independence Ave. SW, Washington, DC 20591, tel. 202/267–3479; Information Hotline, tel. 800/322–7873). Airline policy varies. U.S. carriers allow FAA-approved models bearing a sticker declaring their FAA approval. Because these seats are strapped into regular passenger seats, airlines may require that a ticket be bought for an infant who would otherwise ride free. Foreign carriers may not allow infant seats, may charge the child's rather than the infant's fare for their use, or may require you to hold your baby during takeoff and landing, thus defeating the seat's purpose.

Facilities Aloft   Some airlines provide other services for children, such as children's meals and freestanding bassinets (only to those with seats at the bulkhead, where there's enough legroom). Make your request when reserving. The annual February/March issue of *Family Travel Times* details children's services on dozens of airlines ($10; *see above*). "Kids and Teens in Flight," free from the U.S. Department of Transportation's Office of Consumer Affairs (R-25, Washington, DC 20590, tel. 202/366–2220), offers tips for children flying alone.

Lodging   Children are welcome except in the most exclu-
Hotels   sive resorts; many hotels allow children under 12 or 16 to stay free in their parents' room (be sure to ask the cutoff age when booking). In addition, several hotel chains have developed children's programs that free parents to explore or relax, and many hotels and resorts arrange for baby-sitting.

SuperClubs Boscobel Beach (tel. 800/858–8009) is an all-inclusive resort that specializes in families. Seven-night packages are in the $1,000-

per-person range, and two children under 14 are allowed to stay free if they occupy the same room as their parents. A small army of SuperNannies is on hand to take charge. The activities are scheduled in half-hour periods so children can drop in and out. For younger children there are morning "Mousercises," a petting zoo, shell hunts, and crafts classes; for teens, "Coke-tail" parties at a disco and "No-Talent" shows.

Villa Rentals   Villa rentals are abundant, often economical, and great for families; island tourist boards can usually refer you to the appropriate realtors. When you book these, be sure to ask about the availability of baby-sitters, housekeepers, and medical facilities.

Hints for Travelers with Disabilities

The Caribbean has not progressed as far as other areas of the world in terms of accommodating travelers with disabilities, and very few attractions and sights are equipped with ramps, elevators, or wheelchair-accessible rest rooms. However, major new properties are beginning to do their planning with the needs of travelers with mobility problems and hearing and visual impairments in mind. Wherever possible in our lodging listings, we indicate if special facilities are available.

Lodging   A number of cruise ships, such as the *QE II* and the Norwegian Cruise Line's *Seaward*, have recently adapted some of their cabins to meet the needs of passengers with disabilities. To make sure that a given establishment provides adequate access, ask about specific facilities when making a reservation or consider booking through a travel agent who specializes in travel for people with disabilities (*see below*).

Organizations   Several organizations provide travel information for people with disabilities, usually for a membership fee, and some publish newsletters and bulletins. Among them are the **Information Center for Individuals with Disabilities** (Fort Point Pl., 27–43 Wormwood St., Boston, MA 02210; in MA, tel. 617/727–5540 between 11 and 4 or leave message; outside MA, tel. 800/462–5015; TDD 617/345–9743); **Mobility Internation-**

al USA (Box 10767, Eugene, OR 97440, tel. and TDD 503/343–1284, fax 503/343–6812), the U.S. branch of an international organization based in Britain (*see below*) that has affiliates in 30 countries; **MossRehab Hospital Travel Information Service** (tel. 215/456–9603, TDD 215/456–9602); the **Travel Industry and Disabled Exchange** (TIDE, 5435 Donna Ave., Tarzana, CA 91356, tel. 818/344–3640, fax 818/344–0078); and **Travelin' Talk** (Box 3534, Clarksville, TN 37043, tel. 615/552–6670, fax 615/552–1182).

Travel Agencies and Tour Operators **Tomorrow's Level of Care** (TLC, Box 470299, Brooklyn, NY 11247, tel. 718/756–0794 or 800/932–2012) was started by two Barbadian nurses who develop unique vacation programs tailored to travelers with mobility problems and their families. They can arrange everything from accommodations to entire packages. **Accessible Journeys** (35 West Sellers Ave., Ridley Park, PA 19078, tel. 610/521–0339 or 800/846–4537, fax 610-521-6959) arranges escorted trips for travelers with disabilities and provides licensed caregivers to accompany those who require aid. **Flying Wheels Travel** (143 W. Bridge St., Box 382, Owatonna, MN 55060, tel. 507/451–5005 or 800/535–6790) is a travel agency specializing in domestic and worldwide cruises, tours, and independent travel itineraries for people with mobility impairments.

Publications Two free publications are available from the U.S. Consumer Information Center (Pueblo, CO 81009): "New Horizons for the Air Traveler with a Disability" (include Dept. 608Y in the address), a U.S. Department of Transportation booklet describing changes resulting from the 1986 Air Carrier Access Act and from the 1990 Americans with Disabilities Act, and the Airport Operators Council's *Access Travel: Airports* (Dept. 5804), which describes facilities and services for people with disabilities at more than 500 airports worldwide.

Travelin' Talk Directory (*see* Organizations, *above*) was published in 1993. This 500-page resource book ($35) is packed with information for travelers with disabilities. Twin Peaks Press (Box 129, Vancouver, WA 98666, tel. 206/694–2462 or 800/637–2256) publishes the *Directory of Travel Agencies for the Disabled* ($19.95), listing more than 370 agencies worldwide, and *Wheelchair Vagabond* ($14.95), a collection of personal travel tips. Add $2 per book for shipping.

Hints for Older Travelers

Special facilities, rates, and package deals for older travelers are rare. When planning your trip, be sure to inquire about everything from senior-citizen discounts to available medical facilities. Focus on your vacation needs: Are you interested in sightseeing, activities, golf, ecotourism, the beach? Accessibility is an important consideration. When booking, inquire whether you can easily get to the things that you enjoy.

Organizations The **American Association of Retired Persons** (AARP, 601 E St. NW, Washington, DC 20049, tel. 202/434–2277) provides independent travelers who are members of the AARP (open to those age 50 or older; $8 per person or couple annually) with the Purchase Privilege Program, which offers discounts on hotels, car rentals, and sightseeing. AARP also arranges group tours, cruises, and apartment living through AARP Travel Experience from American Express (400 Pinnacle Way, Suite 450, Norcross, GA 30071, tel. 800/927–0111 or 800/745–4567).

Two other organizations offer discounts on lodgings, car rentals, and other travel products, along with such nontravel perks as magazines and newsletters: The **National Council of Senior Citizens** (1331 F St. NW, Washington, DC 20004, tel. 202/347–8800; membership $12 annually) and **Mature Outlook** (6001 N. Clark St., Chicago, IL 60660, tel. 800/336–6330; $9.95 annually).

Note: Mention your senior-citizen identification card when booking hotel reservations for reduced rates, not when checking out. At restaurants, show your card before you're seated; discounts may be limited to certain menus, days, or hours. If you are renting a car, ask about promotional rates that might improve on your senior-citizen discount.

Educational Travel **Elderhostel** (75 Federal St., 3rd Floor, Boston, MA 02110, tel. 617/426–7788) has offered inexpensive study programs for people 60 and older since 1975. Held at more than 1,800 educational institutions, courses cover everything from marine science to Greek myths and cowboy poetry. Participants usually attend lectures in the morning and spend the afternoon sightseeing or on field trips; they live in dorms on the host campuses. Fees for two- to three-week international trips—including room, board, and transportation from the United States—range from $1,800 to $4,500.

Tour Operators If you want to take your grandchildren, look into **Grandtravel** (*see* Traveling with Children, *above*); **Saga International Holidays** (222 Berkeley St., Boston, MA 02116, tel. 800/343–0273), caters to those over age 60 who like to travel in groups. **SeniorTours** (508 Irvington Rd., Drexel Hill, PA 19026, tel. 215/626–1977 or 800/227–1100) arranges motorcoach tours throughout the United States and Nova Scotia, as well as Caribbean cruises.

Publications *The 50+ Traveler's Guidebook: Where to Go, Where to Stay, What to Do,* by Anita Williams and Merrimac Dillon ($12.95; St. Martin's Press, 175 5th Ave., New York, NY 10010) is available in bookstores and offers many useful tips. "The Mature Traveler" (Box 50820, Reno, NV 89513, tel. 702/786–7419; $29.95), a monthly newsletter, contains many travel deals for older travelers.

Hints for Gay and Lesbian Travelers

Organizations The **International Gay Travel Association** (Box 4974, Key West, FL 33041, tel. 800/448–8550), which has 700 members, will provide you with names of travel agents and tour operators who specialize in gay travel. The **Gay & Lesbian Visitors Center of New York, Inc.** (135 W. 20th St., 3rd Floor, New York, NY 10011, tel. 212/463–9030 or 800/395–2315; $100 annually) mails a monthly newsletter, valuable coupons, and more to its members.

Travel Agencies and Tour Operators The dominant travel agency in the market is **Above and Beyond** (3568 Sacramento St., San Francisco, CA 94118, tel. 415/922–2683 or 800/397–2681). Tour operator **Olympus Vacations** (8424 Santa Monica Blvd., Suite 721, West Hollywood, CA 90069, tel. 310/657–2220) offers all-gay-and-lesbian resort holidays. **Skylink Women's Travel** (746 Ashland Ave., Santa Monica, CA 90405, tel. 310/452–0506 or 800/225–5759) handles individual travel for lesbians all over the world and conducts two international and five domestic group trips annually.

Publications The premier international travel magazine for gays and lesbians is *Our World* (1104 N. Nova Rd., Suite 251, Daytona Beach, FL 32117, tel. 904/441–5367; $35 for 10 issues). **"Out & About"** (tel. 203/789–8518 or 800/929–2268; $49 for 10 issues) is a 16-page monthly newsletter with extensive information on resorts, hotels, and airlines that are gay-friendly.

Credit Cards

The following credit card abbreviations have been used: AE, American Express; D, Discover Card; DC, Diners Club; MC, MasterCard; V, Visa. It's a good idea to call ahead to check current credit card policies.

Arriving and Departing

By Plane

Donald Sangster International Airport (tel. 809/952–3009) in Montego Bay is the most efficient point of entry for visitors destined for Montego Bay, Ocho Rios, Runaway Bay, and Negril. **Norman Manley Airport** (tel. 809/924–8024) in Kingston is better for visitors to the capital or Port Antonio. **Trans Jamaica Airlines** (tel. 809/952–5401) provides shuttle services on the island. Be sure to reconfirm your departing flight a full 72 hours in advance.

Air Jamaica (tel. 800/523–5585) and **American Airlines** (tel. 212/619–6991 or 800/433–7300) fly nonstop daily from New York and Miami; Air Jamaica provides the most frequent service from U.S. cities, also flying in from Atlanta,

Philadelphia, Baltimore, and Orlando. American also flies in from San Juan. **Continental** (tel. 800/231–0856) flies in four times a week from Newark, **Northwest Airlines** (tel. 212/563–7200 or 800/447–4747) has daily direct service to Montego Bay from Minneapolis and Tampa, and **Aeroflot** (tel. 809/929–2251) flies in from Havana. **Air Canada** (tel. 800/776–3000) offers daily service from Toronto and Montreal in conjunction with Air Jamaica, and both **British Airways** (tel. 800/247–9297) and Air Jamaica connect the island with London.

Passports and Visas

Passports are not required of visitors from the United States or Canada, but every visitor must have proof of citizenship, such as a birth certificate or a voter registration card (a driver's license is *not* enough). British visitors need passports but not visas. Each visitor must possess a return or ongoing ticket. Declaration forms are distributed in flight to keep customs formalities to a minimum.

Language

The official language of Jamaica is English. Islanders usually speak a patois among themselves, and they may use it when they don't want you to understand something.

Precautions

Do not let the beauty of Jamaica cause you to relax the caution and good sense you would use in your hometown. Never leave money or other valuables in your hotel room; use the safe-deposit boxes that most establishments make available. Carry your funds in traveler's checks, not cash, and keep a record of the check numbers in a secure place. Never leave a rental car unlocked, and never leave valuables, even in a locked car. Finally, resist the call of the wild when it presents itself as a scruffy-looking native offering to show you the "real" Jamaica. Jamaica *on* the beaten path is wonderful enough; don't take chances by wandering far from it. And ignore efforts, however persistent, to sell you a ganja joint.

Staying in Jamaica

Important Addresses

Tourist Information: The main office of the **Jamaica Tourist Board** is in Kingston (2 St. Lucia Ave., New Kingston, Box 360, Kingston 5, tel. 809/929–9200). There are also JTB desks at both Montego Bay and Kingston airports and JTB offices in all resort areas.

Emergencies **Police, fire, and ambulance:** Police and air-rescue is 119; fire department and ambulance is 110.

Hospitals: University Hospital at Mona in Kingston (tel. 809/927–1620), **Cornwall Regional Hospital** (Mt. Salem, in Montego Bay, tel. 809/952–5100), **Port Antonio General Hospital** (Naylor's Hill in Port Antonio, tel. 809/993–2646), and **St. Ann's Bay Hospital** (near Ocho Rios, tel. 809/972–2272).

Pharmacies: Pegasus Hotel in Kingston (tel. 809/926–3690), **McKenzie's Drug Store** (16 Strand St. in Montego Bay, tel. 809/952–2467), and **Great House Pharmacy** (Brown's Plaza in Ocho Rios, tel. 809/974–2352).

Currency

The Jamaican government abolished the fixed rate of exchange for the Jamaican dollar, allowing it to be traded publicly and subject to market fluctuations. At press time the Jamaican dollar was worth about J$30 to U.S.$1. Currency can be exchanged at airport bank counters, exchange bureaus, or commercial banks. Prices quoted below are in U.S. dollars unless otherwise noted.

Taxes and Service Charges

Hotels collect a 12% government consumption tax on room occupancy. The departure tax is J$200, or approximately $7. Most hotels and restaurants add a 10% service charge to your bill. Otherwise, tips may average 15%–20%.

Guided Tours

Half-day tours are offered by a variety of operators in the important areas of Jamaica. The best
great-houses tours include Rose Hall, Greenwood, and Devon House. Plantations to tour are
Prospect and Sun Valley. The Appleton Estate
Express Tour uses a diesel railcar to visit villages, plantations, and a rum distillery. The increasingly popular waterside folklore feasts are
offered on the Dunn's, Great, and White rivers.
The significant city tours are those in Kingston,
Montego Bay, and Ocho Rios. Quality tour operators include **Martin's Tours** (tel. 809/922–5245),
Tropical Tours (tel. 809/952–1110), **Greenlight
Tours** (tel. 809/952–2650), **SunHoliday Tours**
(tel. 809/952–5629), and **Jamaica Tours** (tel. 809/
952–8074). The highlight of the **Hilton High Day
Tour** (tel. 809/952–3343), which has been
dubbed "Up, Up, and Buffet," is a meet the people, experience Jamaican food, and learn some
of its history day, all on a private estate ($55, in-
cluding transportation). **Helitours Jamaica Ltd.**
offers a way to see Jamaica from the air, with
helicopter tours ranging from 10 minutes to an
hour aloft at prices that vary accordingly ($50–
$250). Contact the Ocho Rios office (tel. 809/
974–2265). **South Coast Safaris Ltd.** has guided
boat excursions up the Black River for some 10
miles (round-trip), into the mangroves and
marshlands, aboard the 25-passenger *Safari
Queen* and 25-passenger *Safari Princess* (tel.
809/965–2513 or, after 7 PM, 809/962–0220).

Getting Around

Taxis   Some but not all of Jamaica's taxis are metered.
If you accept a driver's offer of his services as a
tour guide, be sure to agree on a price *before* the
vehicle is put into gear. All licensed taxis display red Public Passenger Vehicle (PPV) plates,
as well as regular license plates. Cabs can be
summoned by telephone or flagged down on the
street. Taxi rates are per car, not per passenger, and 25% is added to the metered rate between midnight and 5 AM. Licensed minivans are
also available and bear the red PPV plates.

Rental Cars   Jamaica has dozens of car-rental companies
throughout the island. Because rentals can be

difficult to arrange once you've arrived, you *must* make reservations and send a deposit before your trip. (Cars are scarce, and without either a confirmation number or a receipt you may have to walk.) Best bets are **Avis** (tel. 800/331–1212), **Dollar** (tel. 800/800–4000), **Hertz** (tel. 800/654–3131), and **National** (tel. 800/227–3876). In Jamaica, try the branch offices in your resort area or try **United Car Rentals** (tel. 809/952–3077) or **Jamaica Car Rental** (tel. 809/952–5586). You must be at least 21 years old to rent a car (at least 25 years old at several agencies), have a valid driver's license (from any country), and have a valid credit card. Rates average $90 a day.

Traffic keeps to the left in Jamaica, and those who are unfamiliar with driving on the left will find that it takes some getting used to. Be cautious until you are comfortable with it.

Trains The diesel train run by the Jamaica Railway Corporation (tel. 809/922–6620) between Kingston and Montego Bay reveals virtually every type of scenery Jamaica has to offer in a trip of nearly five hours. At press time operation was temporarily suspended.

Buses Buses are the mode of transportation Jamaicans use most, and consequently buses are very crowded and slow. They're also not air-conditioned, and rather uncomfortable. Yet the service is fairly frequent between Kingston and Montego Bay and between other significant destinations. Schedule or route information is available at bus stops or from the bus driver.

Cycles The front desks of most major hotels can arrange the rental of bicycles, mopeds, and motorcycles. Daily rates run from about $45 for a moped to $70 for a Honda 550. Deposits of $100–$300 or more are required. However, we highly recommend that you NOT rent a moped or motorcycle. The strangeness of driving on the left, the less-than-cautious driving style that prevails on the island, the abundance of potholes, and the prevalence of vendors who will approach you at every traffic light are just a few reasons to skip cycles. If you want to adventure out on your own, rent a car.

Telephones and Mail

The area code for all Jamaica is 809. Direct telephone, telegraph, telefax, and telex services are available.

At press time, airmail postage from Jamaica to the United States or Canada was J$1.10 for letters, J90/ for postcards.

Opening and Closing Times

Normal business hours for stores are weekdays 9–5, Saturday 9–6. Banking hours are generally Monday–Thursday 9–2, Friday 9–noon, 2:30–5.

Cruises

Cruising the Caribbean is perhaps the most relaxed and convenient way to tour this beautiful part of the world: You get all of the amenities of a stateside hotel and enough activities to guarantee fun, even on rainy days. Cruising through the islands is an entirely different experience from staying on an island.

Cruise ships usually call at several Caribbean ports on a single voyage but are at each port for only one night. Thus, although a cruise passenger may be exposed to a variety of sightseeing opportunities, and view the geographic and topographic characteristics of several islands, the visits are too quick to get a true feel for each island. A cruise passenger does have the opportunity to select favorite islands for in-depth discovery on a later visit.

As a vacation, a cruise offers total peace of mind. All important decisions are made long before boarding the ship. The itinerary is set in advance, and the costs are known ahead of time and are all-inclusive, with no additional charge for meals, accommodations, entertainment, or recreational activities. (Only tips, shore excursions, and shopping are extra.) A cruise ship is a floating Caribbean resort. For details beyond the basics, given below, see *Fodor's Cruises and Ports of Call 1995.*

When to Go

Cruise ships sail the Caribbean year-round—the waters are almost always calm, and the prevailing breezes keep temperatures fairly steady. Tropical storms are most likely September through November, but modern navigational equipment warns ships well in advance of impending foul weather, and, when necessary, cruise lines vary their itineraries to avoid storms.

Cruises are in high demand—and therefore also higher priced—during the standard vacation times, in winter and around Easter. Some very good bargains are usually available during the immediate postvacation periods such as fall to mid-December, early spring, and the first few weeks after the Christmas and New Year's holidays. Christmas sailings are usually quite full and are priced at a premium.

Choosing a Cabin

Write to the cruise line or ask your travel agent for a ship's plan. This elaborate layout, with cabins numbered, will show you all facilities available on all decks (usually, the higher the deck, the higher the prices). Outside cabins have dramatic portholes or picture-windows that contribute to the romance of cruising, and, though usually sealed shut, most provide expansive sea views. Some windows overlook a public promenade, probably less desirable. Inside cabins are less expensive, but check the plan—you don't want to be over the galley, near the engine room, or next to the elevators. Then check on the facilities offered. Those prone to motion sickness would do best in a cabin at midship, on one of the middle decks. The higher you go, the more motion you'll experience.

Tipping

Although some ships have no-tipping policies, tipping is a major expense on most Caribbean ships. The ship's service personnel depend on tips for their livelihood, and you may feel pressure to help them out. It is customary to tip the cabin steward, the dining-room waiter, the maître d', the wine steward, and the bartender; most cruise lines distribute guidelines with suggested amounts the night before the voyage ends—which is when gratuities are normally given. Figure on tipping about $60 per passenger per week.

Shore Excursions

Tour options, which typically cost $20–$140 per port, are heavily promoted during shore-excursion talks a day or two prior to reaching your post. Better deals are often had by choosing a tour offered by one of the local vendors or renting a car yourself. However, it's always riskier to explore on your own than to leave your one day at port in the hands of the cruise line.

Cruise Lines

To find out which ships are sailing where and when they depart, contact the **Caribbean Tourism Organization** (20 E. 46th St., 4th Floor, New York, NY 10017, tel. 212/682–0435). The CTO carries up-to-date information about cruise lines that sail to its member nations. Full-service and cruise-only travel agencies are also a good source; they stock brochures and catalogues issued by most of the major lines and have the latest information about prices, departure dates, and itineraries. The **Cruise Lines International Association** (CLIA) publishes a useful pamphlet entitled "Cruising Answers to Your Questions"; to order a copy send a self-addressed business-size envelope with 52¢ postage to CLIA (500 5th Ave., Suite 1407, New York, NY 10110).

A complete list of cruise lines that operate in the Caribbean appears below.

American Canadian Caribbean Line (Box 368, Warren, RI 02885, tel. 401/247–0955 or 800/556–7450).
American Family Cruises (World Trade Center, 80 S.W. 8th St., Miami, FL 33130, tel. 800/232–0567).

Carnival Cruise Lines/FiestaMarina Cruises (Carnival Pl., 3655 N.W. 87th Ave., Miami, FL 33178, tel. 305/599–2600).

Celebrity Cruises (5200 Blue Lagoon Dr., Miami, FL 33126, tel. 800/437–3111).

Clipper Cruise Line (7711 Bonhomme Ave., St. Louis, MO 63105, tel. 800/325–0010).

Club Med (40 W. 57th St., New York, NY 10019, tel. 800/CLUB–MED).

Commodore Cruise Line (800 Douglas Rd., Coral Gables, FL 33134, tel. 305/529–3000).

Costa Cruise Lines (World Trade Center, 80 S.W. 8th St., Miami, FL 33130, tel. 800/462–6782).

Crystal Cruises (2121 Ave. of the Stars, Los Angeles, CA 90067, tel. 800/446–6645).

Cunard Line (555 5th Ave., New York, NY 10017, tel. 800/221–4770).

Diamond Cruise Inc. (600 Corporate Dr., Suite 410, Fort Lauderdale, FL 33334, tel. 800/333–3333).

Dolphin/Majesty Cruise Lines (901 South American Way, Miami, FL 33132, tel. 800/532–7788).

Fantasy Cruise (5200 Blue Lagoon Dr., Miami, FL 33126, tel. 800/437–3111).

Holland America Line (300 Elliott Ave. W, Seattle, WA 98119, tel. 800/426–0327).

Norwegian Cruise Line (95 Merrick Way, Coral Gables, FL 33134, tel. 800/327–7030).

Premier Cruise Line (Box 517, Cape Canaveral, FL 32920, tel. 800/473–3262).

Princess Cruises (10100 Santa Monica Blvd., Los Angeles, CA 90067, tel. 310/553–1770).

Regency Cruises (260 Madison Ave., New York, NY 10016, tel. 212/972–4499).

Renaissance Cruises (1800 Eller Dr., Suite 300, Box 350307, Fort Lauderdale, FL 33335, tel. 800/525–2450).

Royal Caribbean Cruise Line (1050 Caribbean Way, Miami, FL 33132, tel. 800/327–6700).

Royal Cruise Line (1 Maritime Plaza, San Francisco, CA 94111, tel. 415/956–7200).

Royal Viking Line (Kloster Cruise Limited, 95 Merrick Way, Coral Gables, FL 33134, tel. 800/422–8000).

Seabourn Cruise Line (55 Francisco St., San Francisco, CA 94133, tel. 800/351–9595).

Seawind Cruise Line (1750 Coral Way, Miami, FL 33145, tel. 800/258–8006).

Silversea Cruises (110 E. Broward Blvd., Fort Lauderdale, FL 33301, tel. 305/522–4477 or 800/722–6655).

Special Expeditions (720 5th Ave., New York, NY 10019, tel. 800/762–0003).

Star Clippers (4101 Salzedo Ave., Coral Gables, FL 33146, tel. 800/442–0551).

Sun Line Cruises (1 Rockefeller Plaza, Suite 315, New York, NY 10020, tel. 800/872–6400).

Windstar Cruises (300 Elliott Ave. W, Seattle, WA 98119, tel. 800/258–7245).

2 Portrait of Jamaica

What is Jerk?

By Helen Willinsky

Born in Jamaica, Helen Willinsky has cooked in hotels and restaurants in Europe and Jamaica. She presently lives in Atlanta and runs her own business. Her cookbook, Jerk: Barbecue from Jamaica, is a helpful introduction to the tastes and techniques of Jamaican cooking.

Jerk cooking is an authentic Jamaican way to cook pork, chicken, seafood, and beef over a fire pit or on a barbecue grill. But it is the special seasoning—a highly spiced combination of scallions, onions, thyme, Jamaican pimento (allspice), cinnamon, nutmeg, peppers, and salt—that makes jerk what it is. To me, jerk cooking is the perfect reflection of the Jamaican lifestyle—spicy, sweet, charismatic, and hot.

The taste of jerked foods is hot with peppers, but, as you savor it, the variety of spices catches up with you, and it is like a carnival where all the elements come together in your mouth. The combination of spices tastes as if they were quarreling and dancing and mingling in your mouth all at the same time. It is not a predictable flavor, but rather a hot, spicy, uncontrolled festival that engages all your senses. It is so unexpected a taste that, in spite of its peppery heat, you automatically want more. We have a saying in Jamaica, "It is very morish"—you want more.

People always ask me, "How did jerk get its name?" I really don't know, but I can tell you almost everyone has a pet theory. Some people say it is called jerk because the meat is turned over and over again—or jerked over and over again—as it cooks over the fire. Others say that is not right; it is called jerk because, when it is served, the jerk man pulls—or, you see, jerks—a portion of meat off the

"What is Jerk?" by Helen Willinsky, was originally published in Jerk, Barbecue From Jamaica and is reprinted by permission of the Crossing Press. Copyright © 1990 by the Crossing Press, Freedom, CA 95019.

pork. To me, it does not matter what it is called, or why. What counts is flavor.

The spices that are used in jerk seasoning have a very special pungency. Jamaican spices are world famous—their oil content is said to be higher than anywhere else in the world, and it is the very oiliness of the spices that intensifies the zip and zest. (It is even said that in World War I, European soldiers were told to line their boots with Jamaican pimento as a way to make their feet warmer in the cold winters.)

Jerk huts are everywhere in Jamaica. You see them clustered by the side of the road, a medley of huts. There is always a wonderful smoky aroma hovering over the huts—the pungency of the burning pimento woods and spices mingling with the delicious scent of the meat. And everywhere are buses, trucks, cars, and vans disgorging hungry passengers in search of jerk pork, jerk chicken, escovitch fish, salt fish and ackee, roast yam, roast plantain, boiled corn, rice and peas, cock soup, mannish water, Irish moss, and festival! Everything that the Jamaicans love is found at the jerk huts, embellished with a great deal of spice. And the cries from each hut: "Which jerk you want?" "Taste mine!"

Jerk huts are usually octagonal or circular, with a telephone pole in the center supporting a thatched or shingled roof. There is a seating bar around the outside of the hut. The food is jerked outside, either in a lean-to attached to the hut, or in a separate hut of its own, or even under a tree. There is rarely any such thing as a parking lot—you park on the side of the road, and you are greeted warmly by the proprietor and the amiable strangers there. You will also see the other customers who are impatiently waiting to sink their teeth into the delicious slabs of meat.

All jerk huts and shacks are very casual affairs, but if it is an especially rustic jerk hut, you can saunter over and pick out what you want directly from the fire. The jerk man or woman will then use a cleaver to slice off whatever you have requested and probably will weigh it to know what to charge you. The meat is served wrapped in foil or on a paper plate. Pork is usually cubed for you on the spot and you stand right there and eat it with your fingers. Chicken tends to be a bit juicier than pork so you really need several napkins to handle that. Usually the meat is very tender because it has been marinated for some time and then cooked slowly. In addition to the pork and chicken, you can get some jerk sausage, and even jerked lobster if you are up on the northern coast of the island.

You must always eat jerk with something sweet or bland to cut the heat—either some festival, a little like a sweet hush puppy, or some hard dough bread, a soft, flat bagel-type bread. Of course, you must cool the mouth with Jamaican Red Stripe beer, Ting greatfruit soda, or a rum concoction. And there is usually music, music, music.

If you are in Jamaica, the best place to look for jerk is in Boston, near Boston Beach, the home of the original jerk pits. The Pork Pit in Montego Bay next to the Casa Montego Hotel (3½ miles from the Montego Bay Airport) and the Ocho Rios Jerk Center (6 Main Street, Ocho Rios) are also famous jerk pits. In Negril, jerk pits line the two main roads that lead in and out of town; in Port Antonio, look for jerk on West Street, near the market.

Jerking pork has been in Jamaica a long time, at least since the middle of the seventeenth century. The method of pit-cooking meat was brought to the island by African hunters who had been enslaved by the British. Quite possibly these West African hunters adapted the seasoning methods of the native Arawak Indians, especially in their use of chile peppers. But it was not until the middle of the eighteenth century, during the guerrilla wars between the escaped ex-slaves, known as Maroons, and England, that there was any real record of this method of preserving pork.

To the Maroon guerrilla bands, the little wild boars that darted through the bush were a wonderful source of food. While some men kept watch on movements of the Redcoats on the plains, others, equipped with long spears, undertook the equally arduous task of pursuing the slippery animals to their lairs in almost inaccessible parts of the mountains.

But caught and killed at last, the boars were brought down from the mountaintops on long sticks to provide food for the weary rebels. Although some meat was eaten at the time of the hunt, most had to be preserved until the next opportunity to hunt presented itself—and who could tell when that would be?

The jerk seasoning combination, laced heavily with salt and peppers, was a means of preservation. The pork was slathered with the aromatic spice combination and wrapped in leaves. Some buried the wrapped marinated pig in a hole in the ground filled with hot stones, and the pork would steam slowly in its own juices. Others would grill it slowly—oh, so slowly, for 12 or 14 hours—over a fire of green wood. This was jerk cooking.

A peace treaty was finally signed by the opposing forces, but jerking pork was now deep in the Jamaican psyche.

Nowadays, it is common to barbecue pork over pimento wood to give the flesh that tangy flavor inherent in the pimento tree; but it was not always so. Those early Maroons used not only the wood of another tree, but also a number of strange herbs to season the meat. The practice was always secret and, even today, if one asked the descendant of a Maroon where his wood and those herbs could be found, he would wave his hand vaguely to the surrounding hills, and say, "Over there."

This wonderful secret way to prepare meat became part of the Jamaican life-style only about 15 years ago. Now there are jerk huts everywhere—in every town, every village, in every city in Jamaica.

Jerking is the latest food craze sweeping the island. It is no longer confined to pork, but now includes fish and chicken. Although jerk pork originally led the field, jerk chicken is now most popular. In Kingston, the capital of Jamaica, the demand for jerk chicken on the weekends is incredible. The steel drums converted to grills are now ubiquitous. They line the streets and, on a weekend in certain sections of Red Hills Road, so much smoke emerges from the line of drums that, except for the smell, one could be forgiven for thinking that a San Franciscan fog had come to Jamaica.

To eat jerk is to feel the influences from which it developed. It is as if you can hear the African, Indian, and calypso cultures that produced it. Jamaicans are great harmonizers— we make delicious soups, we keep our friends forever, we are fantastic musicians and artists—and we have applied this same harmony to our jerk seasoning.

3 Exploring Jamaica

Montego Bay

*Numbers in the margin correspond to points of
interest on the Jamaica map.*

The number and variety of its attractions make
❶ Montego Bay, on the island's north coast, the
logical place to begin an exploration of Jamaica.
Confronting the string of high-rise develop-
ments that crowd the water's edge, you may find
it hard to believe that little of what is now Montego Bay (the locals call it MoBay) existed before the turn of the century. Today many
explorations of Montego Bay are conducted
from a reclining chair on Doctor's Cave Beach,
with a table nearby to hold frothy drinks.

Rose Hall Great House, perhaps the greatest in
the West Indies in the 1700s, enjoys its populari-
ty less for its architecture than for the legend
surrounding its second mistress, Annie Palmer,
who was credited with murdering three hus-
bands and a plantation overseer who was her
lover. The story is told in two novels sold everywhere in Jamaica: *The White Witch of Rose Hall*
and *Jamaica White*. The great house is east of
Montego Bay, just across the highway from the
Rose Hall resorts. *Tel. 809/953–2323. Admission: $10 adults, $6 children. Open daily
9:30–6.*

Greenwood Great House, 15 miles east of Montego Bay, has no spooky legend to titillate visitors, but it's much better than Rose Hall at
evoking the atmosphere of life on a sugar plantation. The Barrett family, from which the English poet Elizabeth Barrett Browning was
descended, once owned all the land from Rose
Hall to Falmouth, and the family built several
great houses on it. The poet's father, Edward
Moulton Barrett ("the Tyrant of Wimpole
Street"), was born at Cinnamon Hill, currently
the private estate of country singer Johnny
Cash. Highlights of Greenwood include oil
paintings of the Barretts, china made especially
for the family by Wedgwood, a library filled with
rare books printed as early as 1697, fine antique
furniture, and a collection of exotic musical in-
struments. *Tel. 809/953–1077. Admission: $7.
Open daily 9–6.*

One of the most popular excursions in Jamaica is **②** rafting on the **Martha Brae River.** The gentle waterway takes its name from that of an Arawak Indian who killed herself because she refused to reveal the whereabouts of a local gold mine to the Spanish. According to legend, she finally agreed to take them there and, on reaching the river, used magic to change its course, drowning herself along with the greedy Spaniards. Her *duppy* (ghost) is said to guard the mine's entrance to this day. Bookings are made through hotel tour desks. The trip is $40 per raft (two per raft) for the 1½-hour river run, about 28 miles from most hotels in Montego Bay. There are a gift shop, a bar-restaurant, and swimming pool at the top of the river where you purchase tickets. To make arrangements call 809/952-0889.

The **Appleton Estate Express** (tel. 809/952-3692 or 809/952-6606), an air-conditioned diesel railcar, takes you through the lush hills and countryside around Montego Bay. You'll get a look at Jamaican villages, plantations growing banana and coconut, coffee groves, and the facility that turns out Appleton Rum. The full-day excursion leaves from the Appleton Estate station every Monday, Thursday, and Friday at 8:50 AM and returns at 4:45 PM. The $70 fare includes transfers to and from your hotel, Continental breakfast prior to departure from the station, buffet lunch, and open bar.

There is also **Mountain Valley Rafting** on the river Lethe, approximately 12 miles (about 50 minutes) southwest of Montego Bay. The trip is $40 per raft (two per raft), lasting an hour or so, through unspoilled hillside country. Bookings are made through hotel tour desks or by calling 809/952-0527.

An Evening on the Great River is a must for tour groups, yet fun nonetheless. The adventure includes a boat ride up the torchlit river, a full Jamaican dinner, a native folklore show, and dancing to a reggae band. *Tel. 809/952-5047 or 809/952-5097. $55 per person with hotel pickup and return; $50 if you arrive via your own transport. Sun., Tues., and Thurs.*

Jamaica

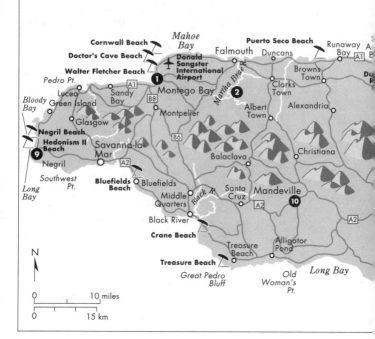

Firefly, **5**
Golden Eye, **4**
Kingston, **11**
Mandeville, **10**
Martha Brae
River, **2**
Montego Bay, **1**
Negril, **9**

Ocho Rios, **3**
Port Antonio, **6**
Port Royal, **12**
Rio Grande
River, **7**
Somerset
Falls, **8**

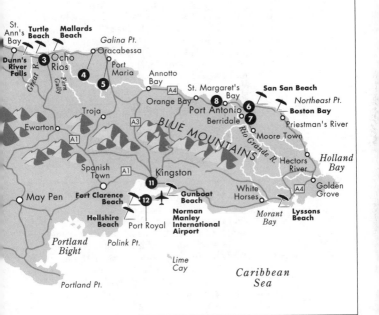

St. Ann's Bay
Turtle Beach
Mallards Beach
Galina Pt.
○ Oracabessa
Dunn's River Falls
3 Ocho Rios
Great R.
Fern Gully
Port Maria ○
Annotto Bay
4
5
○ Troja
A4
Orange Bay ○
St. Margaret's Bay
San San Beach
8
6
Northeast Pt.
Port Antonio
7
Boston Bay
Berridale ○
Priestman's River
A3
Ewarton ○
BLUE MOUNTAINS
Moore Town
Rio Grande R.
A1
Hectors River
Holland Bay
Spanish Town
A1
Kingston
White Horses ○
Golden Grove
May Pen ○
11
A4
Fort Clarence Beach
12
Gunboat Beach
Norman Manley International Airport
Morant Bay
Lyssons Beach
Hellshire Beach
Port Royal
Portland Bight
Polink Pt.
Lime Cay
Caribbean Sea
Portland Pt.

Ocho Rios

3 Perhaps more than anywhere else in Jamaica, **Ocho Rios**—67 miles east of Montego Bay—presents a striking contrast of natural beauty and recreational development. The Jamaicans can fill the place by themselves, especially on a busy market day, when cars and buses from the countryside clog the heavily traveled coastal road that links Port Antonio with Montego Bay. Add a tour bus or three and the entire passenger list from a cruise ship, and you may find yourself mired in a considerable traffic jam.

Time Out | **Double V Jerk Centre** (109 Main St., tel. 809/974–2084) is a good place to park yourself for frosty Red Stripe beer and fiery jerk pork or chicken. It's lively at lunch, when you can tour the adjacent minizoo, with fish and tropical birds.

Yet a visit to Ocho Rios is worthwhile, if only to enjoy its two chief attractions—Dunn's River Falls and Prospect Plantation. A few steps away from the main road in Ocho Rios are waiting some of the most charming inns and oceanfront restaurants in the Caribbean. Lying on the sand of what will seem to be your private cove or swinging gently in a hammock with a tropical drink in your hand, you'll soon forget the traffic that's only a brief stroll away.

The dispute continues as to the origin of the name Ocho Rios. Some claim it's Spanish for "eight rivers"; others maintain that the name is a corruption of *chorreras*, which describes a seemingly endless series of cascades that sparkle from the limestone rocks along this stretch of coast. For as long as anyone can remember, Jamaicans have favored Ocho Rios as their own escape from the heat and the crowds of Kingston.

Dunn's River Falls (tel. 809/974–2857) is an eye-catching sight: 600 feet of cold, clear mountain water splashing over a series of stone steps to the warm Caribbean. The best way to enjoy the falls is to climb the slippery steps. Don a swimsuit, take the hand of the person ahead of you, and trust that the chain of hands and bodies leads to an experienced guide. Those who lead the climbs are personable fellows who reel off bits of local lore while telling you where to stop. *Admission: $3 adults, $1 children.*

Prospect Plantation Tour (tel. 809/974–2058) is the best of several offerings that delve into the island's former agricultural lifestyle. It's not just for specialists; virtually everyone enjoys the beautiful views over the White River Gorge and the tour by jitney (a canopied open-air cart pulled by a tractor) through a plantation with exotic fruits and tropical trees planted over the years by such celebrities as Winston Churchill and Charlie Chaplin. Horseback riding over 1,000 acres is available. *Admission: $10.*

The only major historic site in Ocho Rios is **the Old Fort,** built in 1777 as a defense against invaders from the sea. The original "defenders" spent much of their time sacking and plundering as far afield as St. Augustine, Florida, and sharing their bounty with the local plantation owners who financed their missions. Fifteen miles west is Discovery Bay, site of Columbus's landing, with a small museum of artifacts and Jamaican memorabilia.

Other excursions of note are the one to Runaway Bay's Green Grotto Caves (and a boat ride on an underground lake), a ramble through the Shaw Park Botanical Gardens, a visit to Sun Valley, a working plantation with banana, coconut, and citrus trees, and a drive through Fern Gully, a natural canopy of vegetation filtered by sunlight (Jamaica has the world's largest number of fern species, over 350). Ocho Rios's newest attraction is **Coyaba River Garden and Museum,** featuring exhibits from Jamaica's many cultural influences (the national motto is "Out of Many One People"). The museum covers the island's history from the time of the Arawak Indians up to the modern day. The complex includes an art gallery, crafts shop, and snack bar.

Two area residences are of more than passing interest. **Golden Eye,** just east of Ocho Rios on the main coast road, was used in wintertime by Ian Fleming, the creator of James Bond, from 1946 until his death in 1964. Later Golden Eye served as home to reggae legend Bob Marley and to the founder of Island Records, Chris Blackwell. Today it can be seen only by those who can afford to rent it from the record company. It's an airy complex of deep-blue buildings, walls and bookcases bursting with Bond memorabilia, and a private cove reached by stone steps that would have delighted 007.

⑤ **Firefly,** about 20 miles east of Ocho Rios in Port Maria, was once Sir Noël Coward's vacation residence and is now preserved in all its hilltop wonder by the Jamaican National Heritage Trust. Coward used to entertain jet-setters and royalty in the surprisingly Spartan digs in an Eden-like setting. The Jamaicans who give impromptu tours of Firefly for a cost of $2 used to work for Sir Noël, and they show a moving reverence for his simple grave on the grounds. At press time, plans called for a small theater to be built on the grounds, where Coward's plays will be performed.

Further information on Ocho Rios is available from the Ocho Rios JTB office (tel. 809/974–2570).

Port Antonio

⑥ Every visitor's presence in **Port Antonio** pays homage to the beginnings of Jamaican tourism. Early in the century the first tourists arrived here on the island's northeast coast, 133 miles east of Montego Bay, drawn by the exoticism of the island's banana trade and seeking a respite from the New York winters. The original posters of the shipping lines make Port Antonio appear as foreign as the moon, yet in time it became the tropical darling of a fast-moving crowd and counted Clara Bow, Bette Davis, Ginger Rogers, Rudyard Kipling, J. P. Morgan, and William Randolph Hearst among its admirers. Its most passionate devotee was the actor Errol Flynn, whose spirit still seems to haunt the docks, devouring raw dolphin and swigging gin at 10 AM. Flynn's widow, Patrice Wymore Flynn, owns a boutique in the Palace Hotel and operates a working cattle farm.

Although the action has moved elsewhere, the area can still weave a spell. Robin Moore wrote

The French Connection here, and Broadway's tall and talented Tommy Tune found inspiration for the musical *Nine* while being pampered at Trident.

Recent renovations make a stroll through the town suggest a step into the past. **Queen Street,** in the residential Titchfield area, a couple of miles north of downtown Port Antonio, has several fine examples of Georgian architecture. **DeMontevin Lodge** (21 Fort George St., on Titchfield Hill, tel. 809/993–2604), owned by the Mullings family (the late Gladys Mullings was Errol Flynn's cook), and the nearby **Musgrave Street** (the Craft Market is here) are in the traditional sea-captain style that one finds along coasts as far away as New England.

The town's best-known landmark is **Folly,** on the way to Trident, a Roman-style villa in ruins on the eastern edge of East Harbor. The creation of a Connecticut millionaire in 1905, the manse was made almost entirely of concrete. Unfortunately, the cement was mixed with seawater, and it began to crumble as it dried. According to local lore, the millionaire's bride took one look at her shattered dream, burst into tears, and fled forever. Little more than the marble floor remains today.

Time Out **Navy Island Resort and Marina** is the 64-acre island made famous by Errol Flynn when he bought it. The present operator welcomes visitors, who catch the private launch to his restaurant for lunch (or dinner, by prior reservation: tel. 809/993–2667). Lunch can be as simple as a thick pepper pot soup and grilled fish with lime; dinner can be a five-course spectacular.

❼ Rafting on the **Rio Grande River** (yes, Jamaica has a Rio Grande, too) is a must. This is the granddaddy of the river-rafting attractions, an 8-mile-long swift green waterway from Berrydale to Rafter's Rest. Here the river flows into the Caribbean at St. Margaret's Bay. The trip of about three hours is made on bamboo rafts pushed along by a raftsman who is likely to be a character. You can pack a picnic lunch and eat it on the raft or along the riverbank; wherever you lunch, a vendor of Red Stripe beer will appear at your elbow. A restaurant, bar, and souvenir shops are at Rafter's Rest (tel. 809/993–2778). About $40 per two-person raft.

Another interesting excursion takes you to **8 Somerset Falls,** a special sun-dappled spot crawling with flowering vines where you can climb the 400 feet with some assistance from a concrete staircase. A brief raft ride takes you part of the way. **Athenry Gardens** (tel. 809/993–3740), a 3-acre tropical wonderland, and **Nonsuch Cave** are some 6 miles northeast of Port Antonio in the village of Nonsuch. The cave's underground beauty has been made accessible by concrete walkways, railed stairways, and careful lighting.

A short drive east from Port Antonio deposits you at **Boston Bay,** which is popular with swimmers and has been enshrined by lovers of jerk pork. The spicy barbecue was originated by the Arawaks and perfected by runaway slaves called the Maroons. Eating almost nothing but wild hog preserved over smoking coals enabled the Maroons to survive years of fierce guerrilla warfare with the English.

For as long as anyone can remember, Port Antonio has been a center for some of the finest deep-sea fishing in the Caribbean. Dolphins (the delectable fish, not the lovable mammal) are the likely catch here, along with tuna, kingfish, and wahoo. In October the week-long Blue Marlin Tournament attracts anglers from around the world. By the time enough beer has been consumed, it's a bit like the running of the bulls at Pamplona, except that fish stories carry the day.

Further information on Port Antonio is available from the Port Antonio JTB office (tel. 809/993–3051).

Crystal Springs (tel. 809/993–2609), about 18 miles west of Port Antonio, has more than 15,000 orchids, and hummingbirds dart among the blossoms, landing on visitors' outstretched hands. Hiking and camping are available here. *Admission: 50¢. Open daily.*

Negril

Situated 52 miles southwest of Montego Bay on the winding coast road, **Negril** is no longer Jamaica's best-kept secret. In fact, it has begun to shed some of its bohemian, ramshackle atmosphere for the attractions and activities traditionally associated with Montego Bay. Applauding the sunset from Rick's Cafe may still be the highlight of a day in Negril, yet increasingly the hours before and after have come to be filled with conventional recreation.

One thing that has not changed around this west coast center (whose only true claim to fame is a 7-mile beach) is the casual approach to life. As you wander from lunch in the sun to shopping in the sun to sports in the sun, you'll find that swimsuits are common attire. Want to dress for a special meal? Slip a caftan over your bathing suit.

Negril's newest attraction is the **Anancy Family Fun & Nature Park** (tel. 800/468–6728 or 809/957–4100), just across the street from the family-oriented Poinciana Beach Resort. Named after the mischievous spider character in Jamaican folktales, the 3-acre site features an 18-hole miniature golf course, go-cart rides, a fishing pond, and a nature trail, with more attractions planned. Another new attraction is the **Negril Hills Golf Club.** The 18-hole championship course, designed by Roy Case and Robert Simons, is slated to open by mid-1995.

Even though you may be staying at one of the charming smaller inns in Negril, you may enjoy spending a day at **Hedonism II** (*see* Chapter 7, Lodging), a kind of love poem to health, Mother Nature, and good (mostly clean) fun. The owners love to publicize the occasional nude volleyball game in the pool at 3 AM, but most of the pampered campers are in clothes and in bed well before that hour. And what if Hedonism II is not the den of iniquity it likes to appear to be? What it is, and what your day pass ($50) gets you, is a taste of the spirit as well as the food and drink—and participation in water sports, tennis, squash, and daily activities.

Next to Hedonism II is a sister resort, the **Grand Lido** (*see* Chapter 7, Lodging), that offers a "night pass" for nonguests that includes dinner at the Cafe Lido, live entertainment, and dusk-to-dawn dancing. The price is a hefty $75, and reservations are a must.

Further information on Negril is available from the Negril JTB office (tel. 809/957–4243).

After sunset, activity centers on **West End Road,** Negril's main (and only) thoroughfare, which comes to life in the evening with bustling bistros and earsplitting discos. West End Road may still be unpaved, yet it leads to the town's only building of historical significance, the **Lighthouse.** All anyone can tell you about it, however, is that it's been there for a while. Even historians find it hard to keep track of the days in Negril.

Negril today stretches along the coast south from the horse-shoe-shaped **Bloody Bay** (named during the period when it was a whale-processing center) along the calm waters of **Long Bay** to the Lighthouse section and the landmark **Rick's Cafe** (tel. 809/957–4335). Sunset at Rick's is a Negril tradition. Divers spiral downward off 50-foot-high cliffs into the deep green depths as the sun turns into a ball of fire and sets the clouds ablaze with color.

In the 18th century Negril was where the English ships assembled in convoys for the dangerous ocean crossing. Not only were there pirates in the neighborhood, but the infamous Calico Jack and his crew were captured right here, while they guzzled the local rum. All but two of them were hanged on the spot; Mary Read and Anne Bonney were pregnant at the time, and their execution was delayed.

Mandeville

More than a quarter of a century after Jamaica achieved its independence from Great Britain, ❿ **Mandeville** seems like a hilly tribute to all that is genteel and admirable in the British character. At 2,000 feet above sea level, 70 miles southeast of Montego Bay, Mandeville is considerably cooler than the coastal area 25 miles to the south. Its vegetation is more lush, thanks to the mists that drift through the mountains. The people of Mandeville live their lives around a village green, a Georgian courthouse, tidy cottages and gardens, even a parish church. The entire scene could be set down in Devonshire, were it not for the occasional poinciana blossom or citrus grove.

Mandeville is omitted from most tourist itineraries even though its residents are increasingly interested in showing visitors around. It is still much less expensive than any of the coastal resorts, and its diversions include horseback riding, cycling, croquet, hiking, tennis, golf, and people-meeting.

The town itself is characterized by its orderliness. You may stay here several days, or a glimpse of the lifestyle may satisfy you and you'll scurry back to the steamy coast. **Manchester Club** features tennis, nine holes of golf, and well-manicured greens; **Mrs. Stephenson** conducts photographic tours of her **Gardens** (tel. 809/962–2328), an arboretum filled with lovely orchids and fruit trees; and the natural **Bird Sanctuary** at **Marshall's Penn Great House** (tel. 809/962–2260) is visited by more than 25 species indigenous to Jamaica. Tours of this bird sanctuary are by appointment only and are led by owner Robert Sutton, one of Jamaica's leading ornithologists. Other sites worth visiting are **Lover's Leap,** where legend has it that two slave lovers leapt off the 1,700-foot-high cliff rather than be recaptured by their plantation owner, and the **High Mountain Coffee Plantation** (tel. 809/962–1072 or 809/962–3265) in nearby Williamsfield, where free tours (by appointment only) show how coffee beans are turned into one of American's favorite morning drinks.

Further information on Mandeville is available from the Mandeville office of the JTB (tel. 809/962–1072).

Kingston

The reaction of most visitors to the capital city, situated on the southeast coast of Jamaica, is anything but love at first sight. In fact, only a small percentage of visitors to Jamaica see it at

⑪ all. **Kingston,** for the tourist, may seem as re-
mote from the resorts of Montego Bay as the
loneliest peak in the Blue Mountains. Yet the islanders themselves can't seem to let it go.
Everybody talks about Kingston, about their
homes or relatives there, about their childhood
memories. More than the sunny havens of the
north coast, Kingston is a distillation of the true
Jamaica. Parts of it may be dirty, crowded, often raucous, yet it is the ethnic cauldron that
produces the cultural mix that is the nation's
greatest natural resource. Kingston is a cultural
and commercial crossroads of international and
local movers and shakers, art-show openings,
theater (from Shakespeare to pantomime), and
superb shopping. Here, too, the University of
the West Indies explores Caribbean art and literature, as well as science. As one Jamaican put
it, "You don't really know Jamaica until you
know Kingston."

The first-time business or pleasure traveler may
prefer to begin with New Kingston, which glis-
tens with hotels, office towers, apartments, and
boutiques. Newcomers may feel more comfortable settling in here and venturing forth from
comfort they know will await their return.

Kingston's colonial past is very much alive away
from the high rises of the new city. **Devon House**
(tel. 809/929–7029), our first stop, is reached
through the iron gates at 26 Hope Road. Built
in 1881 and bought and restored by the government in the 1960s, the mansion has period
furnishings. Shoppers will appreciate Devon
House, for the firm Things Jamaican has converted portions of the space into some of the
best crafts shops on the island. On the grounds
you'll find one of the few mahogany trees to
survive Kingston's ambitious but not always
careful development. *Devon House, open
Tues.–Sat. 10–5. Admission: $1.50. Shops open
Mon.–Sat. 10–6.*

Further information on Kingston is available at
the Kingston JTB office (tel. 809/929–9200).

Time Out   Bob Marley's former cook has opened her own
restaurant, on two floors of a simple wooden
rondavel. **Minnie's Ethiopian Herbal-Health**

Food (176 Old Hope Rd., tel. 809/927–9207) sells
food and fresh juices (at last count, there were
more than 15 fresh fruit juices), prepared Rasta
health-food style. From early in the AM, this is
the place for a true Jamaican breakfast of *ackee*
with "festival" (cornmeal bread) or callaloo with
"food" (ground tubers), then on to a lunch of
vegetable run-down (vegetables cooked with coconut milk and spices) or gungo-pea stew. On
Friday nights musicians drop by to jam and
juice.

Among nearby residences, **King's House,** farther along Hope Road, is the home of Jamaica's
governor-general, and **Vale Royal** on Montrose
Road is home to the prime minister. The latter
structure, originally built as a plantation house
in the 1700s, is one of the few still standing in the
capital that has a lookout tower for keeping an
eye on ships in the harbor. *Tel. 809/927–6424.
King's House is only open Mon.–Sat. 10–5.*

Once you have accepted the fact that Kingston
doesn't look like a travel poster—too much life
goes on here for that—you may see your trip
here for precisely what it is, the single best introduction to the people of Jamaica. Near the
waterfront, the **Institute of Jamaica** (tel. 809/
922–0620) is a museum and library that traces
the island's history from the Arawaks to current
events. The charts and almanacs here make fascinating browsing; one example, famed as the
Shark Papers, is made up of damaging evidence
tossed overboard by a guilty sea captain and later recovered from the belly of a shark.

From the institute, push onward to the **University of the West Indies** (tel. 809/927–1660) in the
city's Mona section. A cooperative venture begun after World War II by several West Indian
governments, the university is set in an eye-
catching cradle of often misty mountains. In addition to a bar and a disco where you can meet
the students (they pay dues, while tourists en-
ter free), the place seems a monument to the
conviction and commitment that education lead
to a better life for the entire Caribbean.

Jamaica's rich cultural life is evoked at the **National Gallery** (12 Ocean Blvd., tel. 809/922–

1561), which was once at Devon House and can now be found at Kingston Mall near the reborn waterfront section. The artists represented here may not be household words in other nations, yet the paintings of such intuitive masters as John Dunkley, David Miller, Sr., and David Miller, Jr., reveal a sensitivity to the life around them that transcends academic training. Among other highlights from the 1920s through the 1980s are works by Edna Manley and Mallica Reynolds, better known as Kapo. Reggae fans touring the National Gallery will want to look for Christopher Gonzalez's controversial statue of Bob Marley.

Reggae fans will also want to see **Tuff Gong International** (56 Hope Rd.). Painted in Rastafarian red, yellow, and green, this recording studio was built by Marley at the height of his career. The house has since become the **Bob Marley Museum** (tel. 809/927–9152), with impromptu tours given by just about anyone who may be around. Certainly there is much here to help the outsider understand Marley, reggae, and Jamaica itself. The Ethiopian flag is a reminder that Rastas consider the late Ethiopian emperor Haile Selassie to be the Messiah, a descendant of King Solomon and the Queen of Sheba. A striking mural by Everald Brown, *The Journey of Superstar Bob Marley*, depicts the hero's life from its beginnings in a womb shaped like a coconut to enshrinement in the hearts of the Jamaican people.

While no longer lovingly cared for, the **Royal Botanical Gardens at Hope** (tel. 809/927–1257) is a nice place to while away an afternoon. Donated to Jamaica by the Hope family following the abolition of slavery, the garden consists of 50 acres filled with tropical trees, plants, and flowers, most clearly labeled for those taking a self-guided tour. Free concerts are given here on the first Sunday of each month.

Unless your visit must be very brief, you shouldn't leave Kingston without a glimpse of ⑫ "the wickedest city in the world." **Port Royal** has hardly been that since an earthquake tumbled it into the sea in 1692, yet the spirits of Henry Morgan and other buccaneers add a great deal of energy to what remains. The proudest possession of **St. Peter's Church,** rebuilt in 1725 to replace Christ's Church, is a silver communion plate said to have been donated by Morgan himself.

You can no longer down rum in Port Royal's legendary 40 taverns, but you can take in a draft of the past at the **Archaeological and Historical Museum** (tel. 809/924–8706), located within the Police Training School building, and explore the impressive remains of Fort Charles, once the area's major garrison. On the grounds are a small **maritime museum** and **Giddy House,** an old artillery storehouse that gained its name after being permanently tilted by the earthquake of 1907. Nearby is a graveyard in which rests a man who died twice. According to the tombstone, Lewis Galdy was swallowed up in the great earthquake of 1692, spewed into the sea, rescued, and lived another four decades in "Great Reputation." Port Royal attractions are open daily 9–5.

Jamaica for Free

Sixteen years ago Jamaica introduced the "Meet the People" concept that has become so popular in the Caribbean. One of the best free attractions anywhere, it allows visitors to get together with islanders who have compatible interests and expertise. The nearly 600 Jamaican families who participate in Meet the People on a voluntary basis offer their guests a spectrum of activities from time at a business or home to musical or theatrical performances. The program's theme is Forget Me Not, the name of a tiny blue flower that grows on Jamaican hillsides. Once you've met these people, you're not likely to forget them. It's helpful to arrange your occasion through the Jamaica Tourist Board in advance of your trip.

Off the Beaten Track

The Cockpit Country, 15 miles inland from Montego Bay and one of the most primitive areas in the West Indies, is a terrain of pitfalls and potholes carved by nature in limestone. For nearly a century after 1655 it was known as the Land of

Look Behind because British soldiers rode their horses back-to-back in pairs, looking out for the savage freedom fighters known as Maroons. Fugitive slaves who refused to surrender to the invading English, the Maroons eventually won a treaty of independence and continue to live apart from the rest of Jamaica in the Cockpit Country. The government leaves them alone, untaxed and ungoverned by outside authorities. Minibus tours from Montego Bay to Maroon headquarters at Accompong are offered through the **Maroon Tourist Attraction Co.** (tel. 809/952–4546).

The **Blue Mountains** are lush, with deep valleys and soaring peaks that climb into the clouds. Admirers of Jamaica's wonderful coffee may wish to take a tour to **Pine Grove** or to the Jablum coffee plant at **Mavis Bank.** Unless you are traveling with a local, do not rent a car and go on your own, as the mountain roads wind and dip, hand-lettered signs blow away, and a tourist can easily get lost—not just for hours, but for days. Pine Grove, a working coffee farm that doubles as an inn, has a restaurant that serves owner Marcia Thwaites's Jamaican cuisine. Mavis Bank is delightfully primitive—considering the retail price of the beans it processes. There is no official tour; ask someone to show you around.

If your calf muscles are in good shape, another way to see the **Blue Mountains** is by the downhill bicycle tour offered by Paul and Becky Lemoine (tel. 809/974–0635). The day-long adventure costs $80 and includes lunch. Or visit Gloria Palomino's café restaurant **the Gap** (tel. 809/923–5617; open for lunch Tues.–Sun.), 4,200 feet above sea level, adjacent to several well-defined nature walking trails. Her gift shop sells the coveted Blue Mountain coffee. On your way up (or back) stop in World's End for a free tour of **Dr. Sangster's Rum Factory** (call ahead, tel. 809/926–8888). The small factory produces wonderful liqueurs flavored with local coffee beans, oranges, coconuts, and other Jamaican produce; samples are part of the tour.

Spanish Town, 12 miles west of Kingston on A1, was the island's capital under Spanish rule. The town boasts the tiered Georgian **Antique Square,** the **Jamaican People's Museum of Crafts and Technology** (in the Old King's House stables), and the oldest cathedral (**St. James**) in the Western Hemisphere. Spanish Town's original name was Santiago de la Vega, which the English corrupted to St. Jago de la Vega, both meaning St. James of the Plains.

4 Sports, Fitness, Beaches

Participant Sports

The tourist board licenses all operators of recreational activities, which should ensure you of fair business practices as long as you deal with companies that display the decals.

Fishing

Deep-sea fishing can be great around the island. Port Antonio gets the headlines with its annual Blue Marlin Tournament, and Montego Bay and Ocho Rios have devotees who talk of the sailfish, yellowfin tuna, wahoo, dolphin, and bonito. Licenses are not required. Boat charters can be arranged at your hotel.

Golf

The best courses are found around Montego Bay at **Tryall** (tel. 809/952–5110), **Half Moon** (tel. 809/953–2560), **Rose Hall,** (tel. 809/953–2650), and **Ironshore** (tel. 809/953–2800). Good courses are also found at **Caymanas** (tel. 809/926–8144) and **Constant Spring** (tel. 809/924–1610) in Kingston and at **SuperClubs Runaway Bay** (tel. 809/973–2561) and **Sandals Golf and Country Club** (tel. 809/974–2528), formerly Upton, in Ocho Rios. A 9-hole course in the hills of Mandeville is called **Manchester Club** (tel. 809/962–2403). Great golf and spectacular scenery also go hand in hand at the new **Negril Hills Golf Club** in Negril, which is scheduled to open by early-to-mid 1995. **Prospect Plantation** (tel. 809/974–2058) in Ocho Rios has an 18-hole minigolf course.

Horseback Riding

Jamaica is fortunate to have the best equestrian facility in the Caribbean, **Chukka Cove** (write Box 160, Ocho Rios, St. Ann, tel. 809/972–2506), near Ocho Rios. The resort, complete with stylishly outfitted villas, offers full instruction in riding, polo, and jumping, as well as hour-long trail rides, three-hour beach rides, and rides to a great house. Weekends, in-season, this is the place for hot polo action and equally hot social action. **Rocky Point Stables** (tel. 809/953–2286), just east of the Half Moon Club in Montego Bay,

Rhodes Hall Plantation Ltd., between Green Island and Negril (tel. 809/957–4258), and **Prospect Plantation** (tel. 809/974–2058) also offer rides.

Tennis

Many hotels have tennis facilities that are free to their guests, but some will allow nonguests to play for a fee. The sport is a highlight at **Tryall** (tel. 809/952–5110), **Round Hill Hotel and Villas** (tel. 809/952–5150), **Sandals Montego Bay** (tel. 809/952–5510), and **Half Moon Club** (tel. 809/953–2211) in Montego Bay; **Swept Away** (tel. 809/957–4061) in Negril; and **Sandals Dunn's River** (tel. 809/972–1610), **Sans Souci Lido** (tel. 809/974–2353), and **Ciboney** (tel. 809/974–5503) in Ocho Rios.

Water Sports

The major areas for swimming, windsurfing, snorkeling, and scuba diving are Negril in the west and Port Antonio in the east. All the large resorts rent equipment for a deposit and/or a fee. Diving is perhaps the only option that requires training, because you need to show a C-card in order to participate. However, some dive operators on the island are qualified to certify you. **Blue Whale Divers** (Negril, tel. 809/957–4438), **Sun Divers** (Poinciana Beach Hotel, Negril, tel. 809/957–4069, and Ambiance Hotel, Runaway Bay, tel. 809/973–2346), **Garfield Dive Station** (Ocho Rios, tel. 809/974–5749), **Sea World Resorts Ltd.** (Montego Bay, tel. 809/953–2180, fax 809/952–5018), and **Sandals Beach Resort Watersports** (Montego Bay, tel. 809/979–0104) offer certification courses and dive trips. Most all-inclusive resorts offer free scuba diving to their guests. Some tour operators offer day trips that include an offshore excursion, snorkeling equipment, lunch, and cocktails. **Aqua Action at San San Beach** (tel. 809/993–3318) and **Lady Godiva** (Dragon Bay, tel. 809/993–3281) in Port Antonio both offer scuba diving and snorkeling.

Beaches

Jamaica has some 200 miles of beaches, some of them still uncrowded. The beaches listed below are public places (there is usually a small admission charge), and they are among the best Jamaica has to offer. In addition, nearly every resort has its own private beach, complete with towels and water sports. Some of the larger resorts sell day passes to nonguests. Generally, the farther west you travel, the lighter and finer the sand.

Doctor's Cave Beach at Montego Bay shows a tendency toward population explosion, attracting Jamaicans and tourists alike; at times it may resemble Fort Lauderdale at spring break. The 5-mile stretch of sugary sand has been spotlighted in so many travel articles and brochures over the years that it's no secret to anyone. On the bright side, Doctor's Cave is well fitted for all its admirers with changing rooms, colorful if overly insistent vendors, and a large selection of snacks.

Two other popular beaches in the Montego Bay area are **Cornwall Beach,** farther up the coast, which is smaller, also lively, with lots of food and drink available and a water-sports concession, and **Walter Fletcher Beach,** on the bay near the center of town. Fletcher offers protection from the surf on a windy day and therefore unusually fine swimming; the calm waters make it a good bet for children, too.

Ocho Rios appears to be just about as busy as MoBay these days, and the busiest beach is usually **Mallards.** The **Jamaica Grande** hotel, formerly the Mallards Beach and Americana hotels, is here, spilling out its large convention groups at all hours of the day. Next door is **Turtle Beach,** which islanders consider *the* place for swimming in Ocho Rios.

In Port Antonio, head for **San San Beach** or **Boston Bay.** Any of the shacks spewing scented smoke along the beach at Boston Bay will sell you the famous peppery delicacy, jerk pork.

Puerto Seco Beach at Discovery Bay is a sunny, sandy beach.

There are no good beaches in Kingston. Beach goers can travel outside of the city, but the beaches there, as a rule, are not as beautiful as those in the resort areas. The most popular stretch of sand is **Hellshire Beach** in Bridgeport, about a 20–30 minute drive from Kingston. **Fort Clarence,** a beach in the Hellshire Hills area southwest of the city, has changing facilities and entertainment. Sometimes Kingstonians are willing to drive 32 miles east to the lovely golden **Lyssons Beach** in Morant Bay or, for a small negotiable fee, to hire a boat at the Morgan's Harbor Marina at Port Royal to ferry them to **Lime Cay.** This island, just beyond Kingston Harbor, is perfect for picnicking, sunning, and swimming.

Not too long ago, the 7 miles of white sand at **Negril Beach** offered a beachcomber's vision of Eden. Today much of it is fronted by modern resorts, although the 2 miles of beach fronting Bloody Bay remain relatively untouched. The nude beach areas are found mostly along sections of the beach where no hotel or resort has been built, such as the area adjacent to Cosmo's (*see* Chapter 6, Dining). A few resorts have built accommodations overlooking their nude beaches, thereby adding a new dimension to the traditional notion of "ocean view."

Those who seek beaches off the main tourist routes will want to explore Jamaica's unexploited south coast. Nearest to "civilization" is **Bluefields Beach** near Savanna-La-Mar, south of Negril along the coast. **Crane Beach** at Black River is another great discovery. And the best of the south shore has to be **Treasure Beach,** 20 miles farther along the coast beyond Crane.

5 Shopping

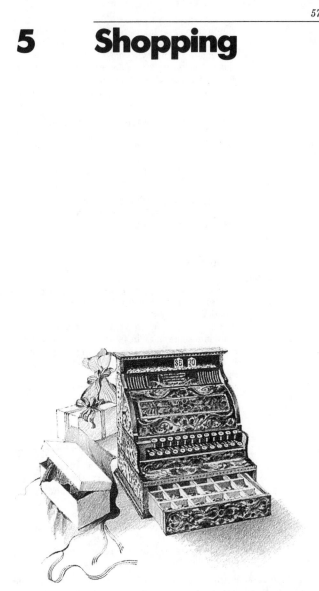

Shopping in Jamaica goes two ways: things Jamaican and things imported. The former are made with style and skill; the latter are duty-free luxury finds. Jamaican crafts take the form of resortwear, hand-loomed fabrics, silk screens, wood carvings, paintings, and other fine arts.

Jamaican rum is a great take-home gift. So is Tia Maria, Jamaica's world-famous coffee liqueur. The same goes for the island's prized Blue Mountain and High Mountain coffees and its jams, jellies, and marmalades.

Some bargains, if you shop around, include Swiss watches, Irish crystal, jewelry, cameras, and china. The top-selling French perfumes are also available alongside Jamaica's own fragrances.

Shopping Areas

Kingston A shopping tour of the Kingston area should begin at **Constant Spring Road** or **King Street.** No matter where you begin, keep in mind that the trend these days is shopping malls, and in Jamaica they caught on with a fever and an ever-growing roster: **Twin Gates Plaza, New Lane Plaza,** the **New Kingston Shopping Centre, Tropical Plaza, Manor Park Plaza,** the **Village,** the **Springs,** and the newest (and some say nicest), **Sovereign Shopping Centre** (tel. 809/927–5955).

A day at **Devon House** (26 Hope Rd., Kingston, tel. 809/929–6602) should be high on your shopping list. This is the place to find old and new Jamaica. The great house is now a museum with antiques and furniture reproductions and the Lady Nugent's Coffee Terrace outside. There are boutiques in what were once the house's stables: a branch of Things Jamaican, Tanning and Turning for leather finds, first-rate furnishings and antique reproductions at Jacaranda, silver and pewter re-creations (many from centuries-old patterns) at the Olde Port Royal, and some of the best tropical-fruit ice cream (mango, guava, pineapple, and passion fruit) at I-Scream.

Montego Bay and Ocho Rios While you should not rule out a visit to the "crafts market" on Market Street in MoBay, you should consider first how much you like pandemonium and haggling over prices and quality. The crafts markets in Ocho Rios are less hectic unless a cruise ship is in port, and the crafts markets in Port Antonio and Negril are good fun. You'll find a plethora of T-shirts; straw hats, baskets, and place mats; carved wood statues; colorful Rasta berets; and cheap jewelry.

If you're looking to spend money, head for **City Centre Plaza, Overton Plaza, Miranda Ridge Plaza, St. James's Place,** and **Westgate Plaza** in Montego Bay; in Ocho Rios, the shopping plazas are **Pineapple Place, Ocean Village,** the **Taj Mahal, Coconut Grove,** and **Island Plaza.** It's also a good idea to chat with salespeople, who can enlighten you about the newer boutiques and their whereabouts.

Specialty Shops

Arts and
Crafts
Silk batiks, by the yard or made into chic designs, are at **Caribatik** (tel. 809/954–3314), the studio of the late Muriel Chandler, 2 miles east of Falmouth. Drawing on patterns in nature, Chandler translated the birds, seascapes, flora, and fauna into works of art.

The **Gallery of West Indian Art** (1 Orange La., MoBay, tel. 809/952–4547 and at Round Hill, tel. 809/952–5150) is the place to find Jamaican and Haitian paintings. A corner of the gallery is devoted to hand-turned pottery (some painted) and beautifully carved and painted birds and jungle animals.

Harmony Hall (an 8-minute drive east on A1 from Ocho Rios; tel. 809/975–4222), a restored great house, is where Annabella Proudlock sells her unique wood Annabella Boxes. The covers feature reproductions of Jamaican paintings. Larger reproductions of paintings, lithographs, and signed prints of Jamaican scenes are also for sale, along with hand-carved wood combs—all magnificently displayed. Harmony Hall is also well known for its year-round art shows by local artists.

Belts, bangles, and beads are the name of the game at the factory of **Ital-Craft** (Shop 8, Upper Manor Park Shopping Plaza, 184C Spring Rd., Kingston, tel. 809/931–0477). Belts are the focus of this savvy operation, but it also produces some intriguing jewelry and purses (many made from reptile skins). While Ital-Craft's handmade treasures are sold in boutiques throughout Jamaica, we recommend a visit to the factory for the largest selection of these belts, made of spectacular shells, combined with leather, feathers, or fur. (The most ornate belts sell for about $75.)

Go to **Patoo** (Upper Manor Park Plaza, Kingston, tel. 809/924–1552) for fine art, folk art, crafts, and collectibles.

Sprigs and Things (Miranda Ridge Plaza, Gloucester Ave., MoBay, tel. 809/952–4735) is where artist Janie Soren sells T-shirts featuring her hand-painted designs of birds and animals. She also paints canvas bags and tennis dresses.

Things Jamaican (Devon House, 26 Hope Rd., Kingston, tel. 809/929–6602, and 44 Fort St., MoBay, tel. 809/952–5605) has two outlets and two airport stalls that display and sell some of the best native crafts made in Jamaica; items range from carved wood bowls and trays to reproductions of silver and brass period pieces.

Bikinis   **Vaz Enterprises, LTD.** Teeny-weeny bikinis, which more than rival Rio's, are designed by **Sonia Vaz** and sold at her manufacturing outlet (77 East St., Kingston, tel. 809/922–9200), at Sandals, and other resorts (*see* Chapter 7, Lodging).

Jewelry   **L. A. Henriques** (Shop 11, Upper Manor Park Plaza, tel. 809/931–0613) sells high-quality jewelry made to order.

Records   Reggae tapes by world-famous Jamaican artists, such as Bob Marley, Ziggy Marley, Peter Tosh, and Third World, can be found easily in U.S. or European record stores, but a pilgrimage to **Randy's Record Mart** (17 N. Parade, Kingston, tel. 809/922–4859) should be high on the reggae lover's list. Also worth checking are the **Record Plaza** (Tropical Plaza, Kingston, tel. 809/926–7645), **Record City** (14 King St., Port Antonio, tel. 809/993–2836), and **Top Ranking Records** (Westgate Plaza, Montego Bay, tel. 809/952–1216). While Kingston is the undisputed place to make purchases, the determined somehow (usually with the help of a local) will find **Jimmy Cliff's Records** (Oneness Sq., MoBay, no phone), owned by reggae star Cliff.

Sandals Cheap sandals are good buys in shopping centers throughout Jamaica. While workmanship and leathers don't rival the craftsmanship of those found in Italy or Spain, neither do the prices (about $20 a pair). In Kingston there's **Lee's** (New Kingston Shopping Centre, tel. 809/929–8614). In Ocho Rios, the **Pretty Feet Shoe Shop** (Ocean Village Shopping Centre, tel. 809/974–5040) is a good bet. In Montego Bay, try **Overton Plaza** or **Westgate Plaza.**

Gift Ideas

Fine Macanudo handmade cigars make sensational gifts. They can be bought on departure at Montego Bay airport (call 809/925–1082 for outlet information). Blue Mountain coffee can be found at **John R. Wong's Supermarket** (1 Tobago Ave., Kingston, tel. 809/926–4811) and the **Sovereign Supermarket** (Hope Rd., tel. 809/927–5955). If they're out of stock, you'll have to settle for High Mountain coffee, the natives' second-preferred brand. If you're set on Blue Mountain, you may try **Magic Kitchen Ltd.** (Village Plaza, Kingston, tel. 809/926–8894).

Jamaican-brewed rums and Tia Maria can be bought at either the Kingston or MoBay airports before your departure. As a general rule, only rum factories, such as Sangster's, are less expensive than the airport stores, and if you buy at the airport there's no toting of heavy, breakable bottles from your hotel.

6 Dining

Sampling the island's cuisine introduces you to virtually everything the Caribbean represents. Every ethnic group that has made significant contributions on another island has made them on Jamaica, too, adding to a Jamaican stockpot that is as rich as its melting pot. So many Americans have discovered the Caribbean through restaurants owned by Jamaicans that the very names of the island's dishes have come to represent the region as a whole.

Jamaican food represents a true cuisine, organized, interesting, and ultimately rewarding. It would be a terrible shame for anyone to travel to the heart of this complex culture without tasting several typically Jamaican dishes. Here are a few:

Rice and Peas. A traditional dish, known also as Coat of Arms and similar to the *moros y christianos* of Spanish-speaking islands: white rice cooked with red beans, coconut milk, scallions, and seasoning.

Pepper Pot. The island's most famous soup—a peppery combination of salt pork, salt beef, okra, and the island green known as callaloo—it is green, but at its best it tastes as though it ought to be red.

Curry Goat. Young goat is cooked with spices and is more tender and has a gentler flavor than the lamb for which it was substituted by immigrants from India.

Ackee and Saltfish. Salted fish was once the best islanders could do between catches, so they invented this incredibly popular dish that joins saltfish (in Portuguese, *bacalao*) with ackee, a vegetable (introduced to the island by Captain Bligh of *Bounty* fame) that reminds most people of scrambled eggs.

Jerk Pork. Created by the Arawaks and perfected by the Maroons, jerk pork is the ultimate island barbecue. The pork (the purist cooks the whole pig) is covered with a paste of hot peppers, pimento berries (also known as allspice), and other herbs and cooked slowly over a coal fire. Many think that the "best of the best" jerk comes from Boston Beach in Port Antonio.

Patties are spicy meat pies that elevate street food to new heights. Although they in fact originated in Haiti, Jamaicans can give patty lessons to anybody.

Where restaurants are concerned, Kingston has the widest selection; its ethnic restaurants offer Italian, French, Rasta natural foods, Cantonese, German, Thai, Indian, Korean, and Continental fare. There are fine restaurants as well in all the resort areas, and the list includes many that are in large hotels.

Dress is casual chic (just plain casual at the local hangouts), except at the top resorts, some of which require semiformal wear in the evening during high season.

Highly recommended restaurants are indicated by a star ★.

Category	Cost*
Very Expensive	over $40
Expensive	$30–$40
Moderate	$20–$30
Inexpensive	under $20

per person, excluding drinks and service charge (or tip)

Kingston

★ **Blue Mountain Inn.** The elegant Blue Mountain Inn is a 30-minute taxi ride from downtown and worth every penny of the fare. On a former coffee plantation, the antique-laden inn complements its English Colonial atmosphere with Continental cuisine. All the classics of the beef and seafood repertoires are here, including steak Diane and lobster thermidor. *Gordon Town, tel. 809/927–1700. Reservations required. AE, MC, V. Expensive–Very Expensive.*

Le Pavillon. Situated just off the Jamaica Pegasus lobby and noted for its afternoon teas, this is *the* place to go for lunch and dinner. The setting is sophisticated, the menu international with a Jamaican flair, and the service top-notch. The wine list is excellent and costly. A value-packed seafood buffet lunch is served on Friday. *Jamaica Pegasus Hotel, tel. 809/926–3690. Reservations required. AE, DC, MC, V. Expensive.*

The Palm Court. Nestled on the mezzanine floor of the Wyndham Kingston, the elegant Palm Court is open for lunch and dinner (lunch is noon to 3 PM; dinner from 7 PM). The menu is Continental, with a heavy Italian accent: tagliatelle Alfredo, with ham and fresh mushrooms; tricolor pasta with shrimp, fish, and lobster; and a seafood kebab. *Wyndham New Kingston, tel. 809/926–5430. Reservations recommended. AE, DC, MC, V. Moderate–Expensive.*

Temple Hall. Located in the hills, 30 minutes from New Kingston, this restaurant has the ambience of a 17th-century plantation house. The menu features home-grown vegetables, meats, and poultry effectively combining Caribbean nouvelle with Jamaican cuisine. *Stony Hill, tel. 809/942–2340. Reservations required. AE, MC, V. Moderate–Expensive.*

Hotel Four Seasons. The Four Seasons has been pleasing local residents for more than 25 years with its cuisine from the German and Swiss schools as well as local seafood. The setting tries to emulate Old World Europe without losing its casual island character. *18 Ruthven Rd., tel. 809/926–8805. Reservations recommended. AE, DC, MC, V. Moderate.*

Ivor Guest House. Serving international and Jamaican cuisines, this elegant yet cozy restaurant has an incredible view of Kingston from 2,000 feet above sea level. Go for dinner, when the view is dramatically caught between the stars and the glittering brooch of Kingston's lights. Owner Hellen Aitken is an animated and cordial hostess. *Jack's Hill, tel. 809/977–0033. Reservations required. AE, MC, V. Moderate.*

★ **The Hot Pot.** Jamaicans love the Hot Pot for breakfast, lunch, and dinner. Fricassee chicken is the specialty, along with other local dishes, such as mackerel run-down (salted mackerel cooked down with coconut milk and spices) and ackee and salted cod. The restaurant's fresh juices "in season" are the best—tamarind, sorrel, coconut water, soursop, and cucumber. *2 Altamont Terr., tel. 809/929–3906. V. Inexpensive.*

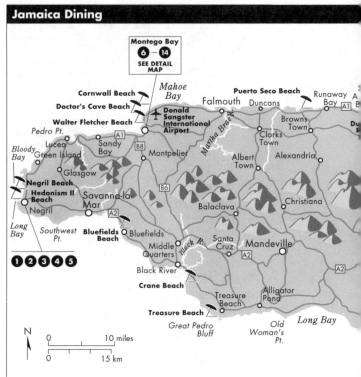

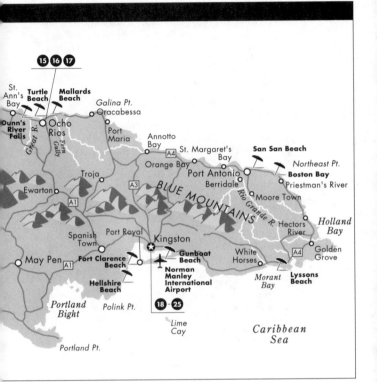

15 **16** **17**

St. Ann's Bay
Turtle Beach
Mallards Beach
Galina Pt.
Oracabessa
Dunn's River Falls
Ocho Rios
Port Maria
Annotto Bay
A4
St. Margaret's Bay
San San Beach
Northeast Pt.
Boston Bay
Priestman's River
Orange Bay
Port Antonio
Berridale
Moore Town
Rio Grande R.
BLUE MOUNTAINS
Troja
A3
Ewarton
A1
Hectors River
Holland Bay
Spanish Town
Port Royal
Kingston
White Horses
Golden Grove
A4
May Pen
A1
Port Clarence Beach
Gunboat Beach
Norman Manley International Airport
Morant Bay
Lyssons Beach
Hellshire Beach
Portland Bight
Polink Pt.
18–**25**
Lime Cay
Caribbean Sea
Great R.
Fern Gully
Portland Pt.

Peppers. This casual outdoor bar is the "in" spot in Kingston, particularly on weekends. Sample the jerk pork and chicken with the local Red Stripe beer. *31 Upper Waterloo Rd., tel. 809/925–2219. MC, V. Inexpensive.*

Montego Bay

Georgian House. A landmark restaurant in the heart of town, the Georgian House occupies a restored 18th-century building set in a shady garden courtyard. An extensive wine cellar complements the Continental and Jamaican cuisines, the best of which are the steaks and the dishes made with the local spiny lobster. Free pickup from Montego Bay hotels. *Union and Orange Sts., tel. 809/952–0632. Reservations required. AE, DC, MC, V. Expensive–Very Expensive.*

Julia's. Couples flock to this romantic Italian restaurant set up in the hills overlooking the twinkling lights of MoBay. Diners choose from an à la carte or four-course fixed-price menu ($34 per person) that includes homemade soups and pastas; entrées of fish, chicken, and veal; and scrumptious desserts. *Bogue Hill, tel. 809/952–1772. Reservations required. AE, MC, V. Expensive.*

★ **Sugar Mill.** Seafood is served with flair at this terrace restaurant. Caribbean specialties, steak, and lobster are usually offered in a pungent sauce that blends Dijon mustard with Jamaica's own Pickapeppa. Other wise choices are the daily à la carte specials and anything flamed. *At Half Moon Golf Course, tel. 809/953–2228. Reservations required for dinner, recommended for lunch. AE, DC, MC, V. Expensive.*

Norma at the Wharf House. This sister property to creative chef and entrepreneur Norma's successful Kingston restaurant has gathered rave reviews as a supper club. Set in a converted 300-year-old stone sugar warehouse on the water, this savvy eatery with blue and white decor offers innovative Jamaican cuisine ranging from Caribbean lobster steamed in Red Stripe beer to jerk chicken with mangoes flambé. Nightly jazz bands enliven the bar and sometimes play out on the wharf. Free pickup service from MoBay-area hotels. Open daily from 9 AM–2 AM.

10 minutes west of MoBay in Reading, tel. 809/ 979–2745. Reservations necessary for dinner. MC, V. Moderate–Expensive.

Pier 1. Despite the fact that it shares a name with the American imports store, Pier 1 writes the book daily on waterfront dining. After tropical drinks at the deck bar, you'll be ready to dig into the international variations on fresh seafood, the best of which are the grilled lobster and any preparation of island snapper. *Just off Howard Cooke Blvd., tel. 809/952–2452. Reservations recommended. AE, MC, V. Moderate– Expensive.*

Town House. Most of the rich and famous who have visited Jamaica over the decades have eaten at the Town House. You will find specials of the day and good versions of standard ideas (red snapper papillot is the specialty, with lobster, cheese, and wine sauce) in an 18th-century Georgian house complete with shuttered windows. The restaurant offers free pickup service from your hotel. *16 Church St., tel. 809/952– 2660. Reservations recommended. AE, DC, MC, V. Moderate.*

Hemingway's Pub. Opened in 1990, this eatery has been a great success with the local business community, which enjoys the pub lunches and dinners. It's an air-conditioned casual bar-restaurant with satellite TV and the added bonus of a terrace for watching the sun go down. *At Miranda Ridge Plaza, Gloucester Ave., tel 809/ 952–8606. No credit cards. Inexpensive.*

★ **Le Chalet.** Don't let the French name fool you. This Denny's look-alike, set in a nondescript shopping mall, serves heaping helpings of some of the best Chinese and Jamaican food in MoBay. Its staff will even pick you up from your hotel. *32 Gloucester Ave., tel. 809/952–5240. AE, MC, V. Inexpensive.*

★ **Pork Pit.** This open-air hangout three minutes from the airport must introduce more travelers to Jamaica's fiery jerk pork than any other place on the island. The Pork Pit is a local phenomenon down to the Red Stripe beer, yet it's accessible in both location and style. Plan to arrive around noon, when the jerk begins to be lifted from its bed of coals and pimento wood. *Adjacent to Fantasy Resort, tel. 809/952–1046. No reservations. No credit cards. Inexpensive.*

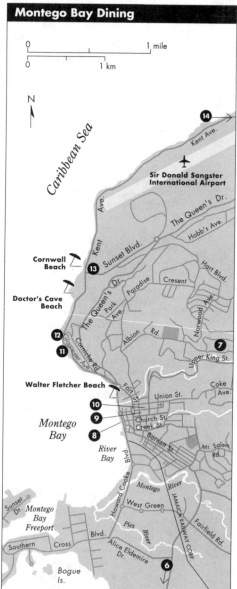

Montego Bay Dining

Negril

Cafe au Lait. The proprietors of Cafe au Lait are French and Jamaican, and so is the cuisine. Local seafood and produce are prepared with delicate touches and presented in a setting overlooking the sea. *Mirage Resort on Lighthouse Rd., tel. 809/957–4471. Reservations recommended. MC, V. Moderate.*

Tan-ya's. This alfresco restaurant is on the edge of the beach of its hotel, Seasplash. It features Jamaican delicacies with an international flavor for breakfast, lunch, and dinner. *Seasplash Hotel, Norman Manley Blvd., tel. 809/957–4041. AE, DC, MC, V. Moderate.*

Rick's Cafe. Here it is, the local landmark complete with cliffs, cliff divers, and powerful sunsets, all perfectly choreographed. It's a great place for a sunny brunch of omelets or eggs Benedict. In the sunset ritual, the crowd toasts Mother Nature with rum drinks, shouts and laughter, and ever-shifting meeting and greeting. When the sun slips below the horizon, there are more shouts, more cheers, and more rounds of rum. *Lighthouse Rd., tel. 809/957–4335. MC, V. Inexpensive–Moderate.*

Cosmo's Seafood Restaurant and Bar. Owner Cosmo Brown has made this seaside open-air bistro a pleasant place to spend a lunch, an afternoon, and maybe stay on for dinner. (He's also open for breakfast. In fact, he only closes from 5 PM to 6:30 PM for a scrub-down.) The fresh fish is the main attraction, and the conch soup that's the house specialty is a meal in itself. There's also lobster (grilled or curried), fish-and-chips, and a catch-of-the-morning. Customers often drop cover-ups to take a beach dip before coffee and dessert and return later to lounge in chairs scattered under almond and sea-grape trees. (There's an entrance fee for the beach alone, but it's less than $1.) *Norman Manley Blvd., tel. 809/957–4330. MC, V. Inexpensive.*

Paradise Yard. Locals enjoy this alfresco restaurant on the Savanna-La-Mar side of the roundabout in Negril. Sit back and relax in the casual atmosphere while eating Jamaican dishes or the house special Rasta Pasta. Open for breakfast, lunch, and dinner. *Tel. 809/957–4006. V. Inexpensive.*

Ocho Rios

★ **Almond Tree.** One of the most popular restaurants in Ocho Rios, the Almond Tree offers Jamaican dishes enlivened by a European culinary tradition. The swinging rope chairs of the terrace bar and the tables perched above a lovely Caribbean cove are great fun. You'll also find pumpkin and pepper-pot soups and fresh fish served in many wonderful ways. *83 Main St., Ocho Rios, tel. 809/974–2813. Reservations required. AE, DC, MC, V. Moderate–Expensive.*

The Ruins. A 40-foot waterfall dominates the open-air Ruins restaurant, and in a sense it dominates the food as well. Surrender to local preference and order the Lotus Lily Lobster, a stir-fry of the freshest local shellfish, then settle back and enjoy the tree-shaded deck and the graceful footbridges that connect the dining patios. *DaCosta Dr., tel. 809/974–2442. Reservations recommended. AE, DC, MC, V. Moderate.*

★ **Evita's.** The setting here is a sensational, nearly 100-year-old gingerbread house high on a hill overlooking Ocho Rios Bay (but also convenient from MoBay). More than 18 kinds of pasta are served here, ranging from lasagna Rastafari (vegetarian) to *rotelle alla Eva* (crabmeat with white sauce and noodles). There are also excellent fish dishes—sautéed fillet of red snapper with orange butter, red snapper stuffed with crabmeat—and several meat dishes, among them grilled sirloin with mushroom sauce and barbecued ribs glazed with honey-and-ginger sauce. *Mantalent Inn, Ocho Rios, tel. 809/974–2333. Reservations required. AE, MC, V. Inexpensive–Moderate.*

7 Lodging

The island has a variety of destinations to choose from, each of which offers its own unique expression of the Jamaican experience. **Montego Bay** has miles of hotels, villas, apartments, and duty-free shops. Although lacking much in the way of cultural stimuli, MoBay presents a comfortable island backdrop for the many conventions and conferences it hosts.

Ocho Rios, on the northeast coast halfway between Port Antonio and Montego Bay, is hilly and lush, with rivers, riotous gardens, and a growing number of upscale resorts, many of which are all-inclusive. Ocho Rios's hotels and villas are all situated within short driving distance of shops and one of Jamaica's most scenic attractions, Dunn's River Falls.

Port Antonio, described by poet Ella Wheeler Wilcox as "the most exquisite port on earth," is a seaside town nestled at the foot of verdant hills toward the east end of the north coast. The two best experiences to be had here are rafting the Rio Grande and a stop at the Trident, arguably the island's classiest resort. Today, Port Antonio enjoys the reputation of being Jamaica's most favored out-of-the-way resort.

Negril, some 50 miles west of Montego Bay, was long a sleepy Bohemian retreat. In the last decade the town has bloomed considerably and added a number of classy all-inclusive resorts (Sandals Negril, Grand Lido, and Swept Away), with a few more on the drawing board. Negril itself is only a small village, so there isn't much of historical significance to seek out. Then again, that's not what brings the sybaritic singles and couples here. The crowd is young, hip, laid-back, and here for the sun, the sand, and the sea.

Mandeville, 2,000 feet above the sea, is noted for its cool climate and proximity to secluded south coast beaches.

The smallest of the resort areas, **Runaway Bay** has a handful of modern hotels and an 18-hole golf course.

Kingston is the most culturally active place on Jamaica. Some of the island's finest business hotels are here, and those high towers are filled with rooftop restaurants, English pubs, serious theater and pantomime, dance presentations, art museums and galleries, jazz clubs, upscale supper clubs, and disco dives.

Jamaica was the birthplace of the Caribbean all-inclusive, the vacation concept that took the Club Med idea and gave it a lusty, excess-in-the-tropics spin. The all-inclusive resort has become the most popular vacation option on Jamaica, offering incredible values with rates from $175–$350 per person per night. Rates include airport transfers; hotel accommodations; three meals a day plus snacks; all bar drinks, often including premium liquors; wine, beer, and soft drinks; a plethora of land and water sports, including instruction and equipment; and all gratuities and taxes. The only surcharges are usually for such luxuries as massages, souvenirs, and sightseeing tours. At times they may feel a bit like Pleasure Island, as all of your needs and most of your wants are taken care of. The all-inclusives have branched out, some of them courting families, others going after an upper crust that would not even have picked up a brochure a few years ago.

If you're the exploring type who likes to get out and about, you may prefer an EP property. Many offer MAP or FAP packages that include extras like airport transfers and sightseeing tours. Even if you don't want to be tied down to a meal plan, it pays to inquire because the savings can be considerable.

Please note that the price categories listed below are based on winter rates. As a general rule, rates are reduced anywhere from 10%–30% from April 30–Dec. 15.

Highly recommended lodgings are indicated by a star ★.

Category	Cost EP*
Very Expensive	over $245
Expensive	$175–$245
Moderate	$105–$175
Inexpensive	under $105

EP prices are for a standard double room for two in winter, excluding 12% tax and any service charge.

Category	Cost MAP**
Very Expensive	over $345
Expensive	$265–$345
Moderate	$130–$265
Inexpensive	under $130

***MAP prices include breakfast and dinner for two daily in winter. Often MAP packages come with use of nonmotorized water sports and other benefits.*

Category	Cost AI***
Very Expensive	over $500
Expensive	$400–$500
Moderate	$335–$400
Inexpensive	under $335

****All-inclusive (AI) winter prices include tax, service, all meals, drinks, facilities, lessons, airport transfers.*

Falmouth

Trelawny Beach Hotel. The dependable Trelawny Beach resort offers seven stories of rooms overlooking 4 miles of beach. Off the beaten path, it's run as a semi-inclusive resort (lunch and liquor are excluded) with an emphasis on families. During the off-season, one child under 15 gets free room and board when sharing accommodations with his or her parents. There's a daily activities program for children, a free shopping shuttle into MoBay, and a designated area of beach for nude sunbathing. *Box 54, Falmouth, tel. 809/954–2450 or 800/223–0888, fax 809/954–2173. 350 rooms. Facilities: 2 dining rooms, 4 lighted tennis courts, pool, complimentary use of water-sports equipment, shopping arcade, beauty salon, disco, nightly entertainment. AE, DC, MC, V. MAP, FAP. Expensive.*

★ **Fisherman's Inn Dive Resort.** A charming red-

Jamaica Lodging

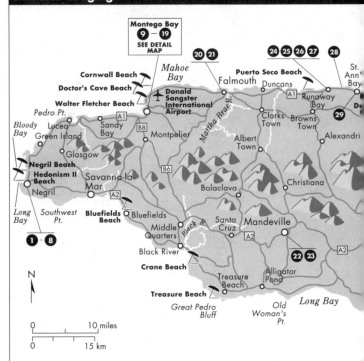

Montego Bay
9 – 19
SEE DETAIL MAP

20 21

24 25 26 27 28

Mahoe Bay

Cornwall Beach
Doctor's Cave Beach
Walter Fletcher Beach

Pedro Pt.

Bloody Bay

Lucea   Green Island

Glasgow

Negril Beach
Hedonism II Beach

Savanna-la-Mar

Negril

Long Bay   *Southwest Pt.*

N

1 – 8

Donald Sangster International Airport

Sandy Bay

Montpelier

A1
B8
B6

Puerto Seco Beach

Falmouth   Duncans   Runaway Bay

Clarks Town   Browns Town

Albert Town

Balaclava

Santa Cruz

Mandeville

Middle Quarters

Black River

Martha Brae R.

St. Ann Bay

De

29

Alexandri

Christiana

22 23

A2

A2

Bluefields Beach   Bluefields

Crane Beach

Black R.

Treasure Beach

Treasure Beach

Great Pedro Bluff

Alligator Pond

Old Woman's Pt.

Long Bay

0   10 miles
0   15 km

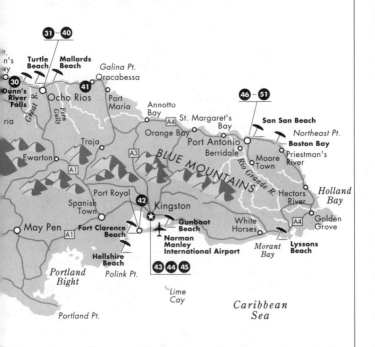

tile-and-stucco building fronts a phosphorescent lagoon at this welcoming hotel run by divers for divers. At night the hotel restaurant offers a free boat ride to diners; dip your hand in the water, and the bioluminescent microorganisms glow. It's really a treat. The bright breezy rooms all face the water, with air-conditioning, satellite TV, patio, and full bath. A great bargain, whether you dive (excellent packages are available) or not. Rates include three dives daily and MAP meal plan; nondiving spouses or mates do get a slight discount. *Falmouth P.O., tel. and fax 809/954–3427. 12 rooms. Facilities: restaurant, bar, pool, water sports (include PADI dive shop). AE, MC, V. MAP. Moderate.*

Kingston

★ **Jamaica Pegasus.** The Jamaica Pegasus is one of two fine business hotels in the New Kingston area. The 17-story complex near downtown boasts an efficient and accommodating staff, meeting rooms, a top-notch restaurant and a hearty café, handsome Old World decor, a pampering ambience, and an international crowd in the lobby. The Polo Bar Lounge in the hotel lobby is a comfortable place to sit and have a drink. Advantages here include an excellent business center, duty-free shops, and 24-hour room service. *Box 333, Kingston, tel. 809/926–3690 or 800/225–5843, fax 809/929–4062. 397 rooms, 16 suites. Facilities: restaurants, cocktail lounge, meeting rooms for 1,000, audiovisual services, shops, Olympic-size pool, jogging track, health club, 2 lighted tennis courts. AE, DC, MC, V. EP, MAP. Expensive.*

Morgan's Harbour Hotel, Beach Club, and Yacht Marina. A favorite of the sail-into-Jamaica set, this small property boasts 22 acres of beachfront at the very entrance to the old pirate's town. Rooms are decorated in either a provincial or 18th-century nautical style that the pirate Captain Morgan would have appreciated. *Port Royal, Kingston, tel. 809/924–8464 or 800/JAMAICA, fax 809/924–8562. 66 rooms. Facilities: restaurant, pier bar, full-service marina, disco, access to Lime Cay and other cays. AE, MC, V. EP. Moderate.*

Wyndham New Kingston. The main competition to the Jamaica Pegasus on the Kingston business beat, the high-rise Wyndham New Kingston also has 17 stories but adds seven cabana buildings. A renovation in 1993 upgraded the facilities; the pleasant modern rooms all include air-conditioning, satellite TV, direct-dial phone, and hair dryer. *Box 112, Kingston, tel. 809/926–5430 or 800/JAMAICA; fax 809/929–7439. 300 rooms, 14 1-bedroom suites. Facilities: 2 restaurants, bars, Olympic-size pool, gardens, conference space for 800, meeting rooms, business center, 2 lighted tennis courts, health club, disco. AE, DC, MC, V. EP, MAP. Moderate.*

Mandeville

★ **Astra Hotel.** A hotel with guest-house charm, the Astra is situated 2,000 feet up in the hills, providing an ideal getaway for nature lovers and outdoors enthusiasts. *Ward Ave., Box 60, Mandeville, tel. 809/962–3265 or 800/JAMAICA, fax 809/962–1461. 22 rooms. Facilities: restaurant and bar, pool, golf course and tennis court nearby, horseback riding, bird-watching, sauna, satellite TV. AE, V. EP. Inexpensive.*

Mandeville Hotel. The Victorian Mandeville Hotel, set in tropical gardens, has redecorated for the 1990s. Rooms are simple and breeze-cooled; breakfast and lunch are served in a new flower-filled garden terrace. *Box 78, Mandeville, tel. 809/962–2460, fax 809/962–0700. 62 rooms. Facilities: restaurant, cocktail lounge, golf privileges at nearby Manchester Club. AE, MC, V. EP. Inexpensive.*

Montego Bay

★ **Half Moon Club.** For four decades the 400-acre Half Moon Club resort has been a destination unto itself with a reputation for doing the little things right. Although it has mushroomed from 30 to over 200 units, it has maintained its intimate, luxurious feel. The rooms, suites, and villas, whether in modern or Queen Anne style, are decorated in exquisite taste, with marvelous touches like Oriental throw rugs and antique radios. Several villas have their own pools. *Box 80,*

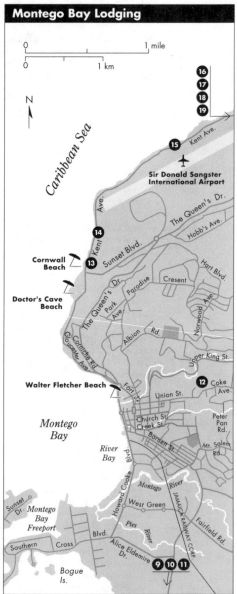

Montego Bay Lodging

*east of Montego Bay (7 mi), tel. 809/953–2211 or
800/227–3237, fax 809/953–2731. 53 rooms, 159
suites and villas. Facilities: 3 restaurants, 3
bars, golf course, 4 squash courts, 13 tennis
courts (7 lighted), horseback riding, health spa,
water-sports center, 19 pools, children's pool.
AE, DC, MC, V. EP, MAP, FAP, All-inclusive.
Very Expensive.*

★ **Round Hill.** Eight miles west of town on a hilly
peninsula, this peaceful resort is popular with
the Hollywood set. Twenty-seven villas housing
74 suites are scattered over 98 acres, and each
villa has a maid who cooks breakfast. There are
also 36 hotel rooms in a two-story building overlooking the sea. The refined rooms all feature
mahogany furnishings and terra-cotta floors.
The privately owned villas vary in decor, but
jungle motifs are a favorite. *Box 64, Montego
Bay, tel. 809/952–5150 or 800/237–3237, fax 809/
952–2505. 36 rooms, 74 villa suites. Facilities:
restaurant, pool, 5 lighted tennis courts, spa
and fitness center, nearby horseback riding,
water-sports center. AE, DC, MC, V. EP,
MAP, FAP, All-inclusive. Very Expensive.*

Tryall Golf, Tennis, and Beach Club. Part of a
posh residential development 12 miles west of
Montego Bay, Tryall clings to a hilltop overlooking the golf course and the Caribbean. Here you
choose between accommodations in the former
great house of a 3,000-acre island plantation and
one of the private villas dotting the landscape,
each with its own pool. *Box 1206, Sandy Bay,
Hanover, Montego Bay, tel. 809/952–5110 or
800/237–3237, fax 809/952–0401. 52 rooms, 41
villas. Facilities: 2 restaurants, golf course, 9
tennis courts (5 lighted), pool with swim-up
bar, water sports. AE, DC, MC, V. EP, MAP,
FAP, All-inclusive. Very Expensive.*

★ **Sandals Royal Caribbean.** Another all-inclusive
resort for couples only, the Royal Caribbean is
enlivened by Jamaican-style architecture arranged in a semicircle around attractive gardens. It's a sister in both theme and quality to
other Sandals resorts; the renovated rooms feature king-size beds, hair dryers, safes, clock radios, and satellite TVs. While sportive and
activity-laden, this property is a bit quieter and
more genteel than the other Sandals and draws
a nicely mixed international crowd. *Box 167,*

*Montego Bay, tel. 809/953–2231 or 800/SAN-
DALS, fax 809/953–2788. 190 rooms. Facilities:
4 restaurants, 3 bars, 3 pools, 4 Jacuzzis, gym,
body shop, disco, private offshore island, beach,
2 lighted tennis courts, putting green, satellite
TV. AE, DC, MC, V. All-inclusive. Expensive.*

Sandals Montego Bay. The largest private beach
in Montego Bay is the spark that lights Sandals,
one of the most popular couples resorts in the
Caribbean. The all-inclusive format includes
airport transfers, all taxes and tips, a plethora
of water and land sports, including scuba diving
and golfing (greens fees included), all sports
equipment and lessons, aerobics classes, meals,
theme parties, and other entertainment. It's a
bit like a cruise ship that remains in port, with
rooms overlooking the bay. The revelers don't
seem to mind the zooming planes (the airport is
next door), and the atmosphere here remains
one of a great big fun party. *Box 100, Montego
Bay, tel. 809/952–5510 or 800/SANDALS, fax
809/952–0816. 243 rooms. Facilities: 3 restaurants, 4 bars, 2 pools, swim-up bar, 4 Jacuzzis,
gym, body shop, water-sports center, 4 lighted
tennis courts, racquetball court, nightclub, satellite TV. AE, DC, MC, V. All-inclusive. Moderate–Expensive.*

Holiday Inn Rose Hall. Here the great equalizer
of hotel chains has done much to raise a run-
down campground to the level of a full-service
property with activities day and night and many
tour facilities. It's big and noisy, with drab hall-
ways and public areas, though the rooms are
cheerful enough. The quietest rooms are those
farthest from the pool. The beach is just a sliver,
but there's live entertainment nightly. *Box 480,
Montego Bay, tel. 809/953–2485 or 800/352–
0731 or 800/HOLIDAY, fax 809/953–2840. 516
rooms, 5 suites. Facilities: 3 restaurants, 4
bars, pool, water-sports center, exercise room, 4
tennis courts, game room, disco, shops. AE,
DC, MC, V. EP. Moderate.*

★ **Richmond Hill Inn.** The hilltop Richmond Hill
Inn, a quaint, daintily decorated 200-year-old
great house originally owned by the Dewars
clan, attracts repeat visitors by providing spectacular views of the Caribbean and a great deal
of peace in the midst of MoBay's hustle. *Union
St., Box 362, Montego Bay, tel. 809/952–3859 or*

800/423–4095. 23 rooms, 5 suites. Facilities: terrace dining room, coffee shop, bar, pool, free beach shuttle. AE, MC, V. EP, MAP. FAP. Moderate.

Wyndham Rose Hall. The veteran Wyndham Rose Hall, a self-contained resort built on the 400-acre Rose Hall Plantation, mixes recreation with a top-flight conference setup. A typical bustling business hotel popular with groups, it has all the amenities and completed a $30 million renovation in 1993. A "Kid's Klub" with daily supervised activities was also added. *Box 999, Montego Bay, tel. 809/953–2650 or 800/996–3426, fax 809/953-5617. 489 rooms, 19 suites. Facilities: 4 restaurants, coffee shop, 3 pools, water sports, 6 tennis courts, golf course, nightclub, lounge, 8 meeting rooms, audiovisual equipment, fitness center, laundry service, shopping arcade. AE, DC, MC, V. EP, MAP, All-inclusive. Moderate.*

Fantasy Resort. After a brief stint as an all-inclusive resort, this property has gone back to normal hotel status. The resort sports high-rise design and a Mediterranean flair. All nine stories have terraces with ocean views. A small beach is across the street. Efficient and pleasant, Fantasy is a good buy, usually booked solid with tour groups. *Opposite Cornwall Beach, Box 161, Montego Bay, tel. 809/952–4150 or 800/223–9815, fax 809/952–3637. 119 rooms. Facilities: dining room, open-air bar, pool, disco, shopping arcade. AE, DC, MC, V. EP. Inexpensive.*

Reading Reef Club. Four miles west of Montego Bay airport, this owner-operated resort is ideal for families and budget-minded honeymooners. Another of Jamaica's fine small-hotel values, it offers simply but tastefully furnished rooms and an excellent pasta and seafood restaurant, the Safari. Golf and horseback riding can be arranged. *Box 225, Reading, Montego Bay, tel. 809/952–5909 or 800/223–6510, fax 809/952–7217. 30 rooms, suites and apartments. Facilities: gourmet restaurant, private beach, pool, dive shop, water sports. AE, MC, V. EP, CP, BP, MAP. Inexpensive.*

Sandals Inn. The Inn is less expensive than the other couples-only Sandals resorts, because it's the only one not on a private beach. It is more intimate than the other Sandals—managed more like a small hotel than a large resort. The charming rooms are smallish, but have balconies facing the pool. There's plenty to do here, but couples in search of more action can enjoy the other two MoBay Sandals by hopping aboard the free hourly shuttle. The in-town location makes the Inn convenient to shopping and tours. *Box 412, Montego Bay, tel. 809/952–4140 or 800/SANDALS; fax 809/952–6913. 52 rooms. Facilities: beach privileges, pool, 2 restaurants, pub, satellite TV, gift shop, lighted tennis court, fitness center. AE, DC, MC, V. All-inclusive. Inexpensive.*

Negril

★ **Grand Lido.** The opening of the SuperClubs' all-inclusive Grand Lido in 1989 broke new ground by extending this popular concept to the upper-income bracket. The dramatic entrance of marble floors and columns sets a tone of striking elegance. The well-appointed oceanfront rooms (split-level and arguably the most spacious and stylish of the all-inclusives), sports facilities, and 24-hr room service follow up in high style. For some, the pièce de résistance is a sunset cruise on the resort's 147-foot yacht, *Zien,* which was a wedding gift from Aristotle Onassis to Prince Rainier and Princess Grace of Monaco and is now captained by Wynn Jones. Grand Lido attracts a slightly more mature and settled crowd than does the usual Negril resort. The gourmet restaurant, Piacere, is one of Jamaica's best, and an atmosphere of cool elegance prevails throughout. *Box 88, Negril, tel. 809/957–4010 or 800/859–7873, fax 809/957–4317. 200 suites. Facilities: 3 specialty restaurants, satellite TV, 24-hr room service, water-sports center including scuba diving, pools, clothed and nude beaches, 4 tennis courts (2 lighted), gym, beauty salon. AE, DC, MC, V. All-inclusive. Very Expensive.*

Sandals Negril. Sandals, built from the best parts of the old Sundowner and Coconut Cove resorts on one of the best stretches of Negril's 7-mile beach, was designed for fun-loving couples seeking an upscale, sportive getaway on a fabulous beach and a casual atmosphere (you can wear shorts to dinner) within an exclusive environment. Water sports, including scuba diving, are emphasized here; and the capable staff is happy to both teach neophytes and take out guests who are already certified. There's an offshore island, a huge swim-up pool bar, and a range of spacious accommodations. Both rooms and staff are sunny and appealing. *Negril, tel. 809/957–4216 or 800/SANDALS; Unique Vacations, 7610 S.W. 61st St., Miami, FL 33143. 199 rooms. Facilities: 3 restaurants, 2 pools, swim-up bar, private island, water-sports center including scuba diving, squash and racquetball courts, 4 tennis courts, croquet lawn, waterskiing, Jacuzzis, saunas, fitness center, movies, satellite TV, disco, piano bar. AE, DC, MC, V. All-inclusive. Expensive.*

★ **Swept Away.** One of the newer and better all-inclusive resorts, Swept Away opened in early 1990 and is geared toward fitness and health-conscious couples, with an emphasis on sports and healthy cuisine. There are 130 suites in 26 cottages; all have a private inner-garden atrium. There are also four two-bedroom villas spread out along a half-mile of "drop-dead" beach. The 10-acre sports complex across the road outclasses the competition by a long shot; the Feathers Continental Restaurant here is open to nonguests. The compound's chefs concentrate on healthful dishes with lots of fish, white meat, fresh fruits, and veggies. *Long Bay, Negril, tel. 809/957–4061 or 800/545–7937; fax 809/957–4060. 138 rooms. Facilities: 2 restaurants, 2 bars, 10 lighted tennis courts, 2 squash courts, 2 racquetball courts, fitness center, steam rooms and saunas, Jacuzzis, pool with lap lines. Full water-sports center including scuba diving. AE, MC, V. All-inclusive. Expensive.*

★ **Hedonism II.** Here is the resort that introduced the Club Med–style all-inclusive to Jamaica a little over 16 years ago. Still wildly successful, Hedonism appeals most to vacationers who like a robust mix of physical activities, all listed daily on a chalkboard. A $2 million refurbishment in 1993 spruced up the public areas; the rooms are modern and handsome, with a lot of blond woods (but the 60% single clientele spends little time in them). *Box 25, Negril, tel. 809/957–4200 or 800/*

859–7873, fax 809/957–4289. 280 rooms. Facilities: open-air buffet dining room, disco, and bar; water-sports center, including scuba diving; fitness center and trapeze and trampoline clinics; horseback riding; 6 lighted tennis courts; shuffleboard; volleyball; squash. AE, MC, V. All-inclusive. Moderate–Expensive.

★ **Charela Inn.** Intimacy is special at the Charela Inn, where each of the quiet, elegantly appointed rooms offers a balcony or a covered patio. The owners' French-Jamaican roots find daily expression in the kitchen, and there's an excellent selection of wines. *Box 33, Negril, Westmoreland, tel. 809/957–4277 or 800/423–4095, fax 809/957–4414. 38 air-conditioned rooms, 1 apartment. Facilities: restaurant, pool, beach. DC, MC, V. EP, MAP. Moderate.*

Negril Gardens. A study in colonial pink and white, with half the rooms beachside and half across the street overlooking the pool. At press time, all of the rooms were in the midst of being refurbished, and a fitness center was being added. *Negril, Westmoreland, tel. 809/957–4408 or 800/752–6824, fax 809/957–4374. 54 rooms. Facilities: terrace restaurant, tennis, beach, pool, water sports, disco. AE, MC, V. EP. Moderate.*

Negril Inn. The rooms in this all-inclusive inn are air-conditioned, and each has a garden view and a patio or balcony. Air-conditioning is about the only modern convenience in this simple place, since rooms do not have phones or televisions. If you don't mind this bit of isolation, you can enjoy the inn's beach—one of the prettiest palm-speckled sandy beaches in Jamaica. *Negril, tel. 809/957–4370 or 800/634–7456, fax 809/957–4365. 46 rooms. Facilities: restaurant, dancing, entertainment, lounge, disco, 2 tennis courts, pool, Jacuzzi, water-sports center. AE, MC, V. All-inclusive. Moderate.*

Negril Cabins. The 12 timber cottages are nestled amid lush vegetation and towering royal palms. The rooms are unadorned, but warm and snug, with a fresh, natural look. The gleaming beach is right across the road. A most convivial place, highly popular with young Europeans. *Negril, tel. 809/957–4350 or 800/423–4095, fax 809/957–4381. 24 rooms. Facilities: restaurant, bar. AE, MC, V. EP. Inexpensive.*

Ocho Rios

★ **Jamaica Inn.** This vintage property is a special favorite of the privileged from both the United States and Europe, a clientele fascinated by the combination of class and quiet. There are weeks in season when every single guest is on at least his or her second visit. Each room has its own veranda (larger than most hotel rooms) on the powdery champagne-color beach. This is the kind of retreat that makes Americans yearn to be colonists again, happily discussing the royals' latest trials. The owning Morrow brothers are committed to making everything perfect; they're not far off. *Box 1, Ocho Rios, tel. 800/ 243-9420 or 809/974-2514, fax 809/974-2449. 45 rooms. Facilities: restaurant, bar, pool, golf, tennis and horseback riding nearby. No children under 14. AE, MC, V. EP, MAP, FAP. Very Expensive.*

Plantation Inn. This plantation actually looks like one—the Deep South variety à la *Gone with the Wind.* The whole place serves up a veranda-soft existence. All the rooms come with private balconies, and each has a dramatic view down to the sea. *Box 2, Ocho Rios, tel. 809/974-5601 or 800/752-6824, fax 809/974-5912. 77 rooms. Facilities: dining and dancing by candlelight, shops, 2 lighted tennis courts, health club, afternoon tea, entertainment twice weekly. No children under 12. AE, DC, MC, V. EP, MAP, FAP, All-inclusive. Very Expensive.*

★ **Sans Souci Lido.** The newest acquistion of the SuperClubs, this pastel-pink cliffside fantasyland looks and feels like a dream, if indeed the dreamer had absolute taste and no need to fret over the bill (unlike the owners, who recently completed a $7 million renovation). Cuisine at the Casanova Restaurant delights resort guests, as does the pampering they get at Charlie's Spa in the form of a complimentary massage, facial, manicure, and pedicure. This elegant, exclusive property is first-rate. A wonderfully luxurious experience. *Ocho Rios, tel. 809/974-2353 or 800/859-7873, fax 809/974-2544. 13 rooms, 98 suites. Facilities: 2 restaurants, full-service health spa and fitness center, freshwater and mineral pool, 3 lighted tennis* *courts, scuba diving, water-sports center. AE, DC, MC, V. All-inclusive. Very Expensive.*

Ciboney, Ocho Rios. A Radisson Villa, Spa and Beach Resort, this stately plantation property opened its doors in winter 1991. The $46 million project has 36 rooms in a plantation-style great house and 264 spacious one-, two-, and three-bedroom villa suites on 45 lush hillside acres overlooking the Caribbean. It is operated as a luxury all-inclusive geared toward affluent adults, both singles and couples; no children under the age of 16 are allowed. Outstanding features are the European-style spa and four signature restaurants, including the Orchids restaurant, whose menu was developed by the Culinary Institute of America. Every villa has a private attendant and pool, giving guests the ultimate in privacy and pampering. All guests receive complimentary massage, foot reflexology, manicure, and pedicure. *Box 728, Main St., Ocho Rios, tel. 809/974–1027 or 800/333–3333, fax 809/974–5838. 264 1-, 2-, and 3-bedroom suites, 36 rooms. Facilities: 4 restaurants, 2 pools with swim-up bars, 6 tennis courts, full-service spa, steam room, sauna, hot tubs, cold plunges, golf greens fees and transportation, 3 bars, 2 squash courts, racquetball court, water-sports center including scuba diving, beach shuttle to private beach club, disco, boutique, beauty salon, jogging track, nightly entertainment, conference facilities. All-inclusive. Expensive–Very Expensive.*

★ **Boscobel Beach.** Boscobel Beach is a parent's dream for a Jamaican vacation, an all-inclusive that makes families feel welcome. Everybody is kept busy all week for a single package price, and everyone leaves happy. The cheery day-care centers, divided by age group, should be a model for the rest of the Caribbean. Thoughtfully, there is an "adults only" section (for when the kids want to get away). *Box 63, Ocho Rios, tel. 809/974–3291 or 800/859–7873, fax 809/975–3270. 208 rooms, half of them junior suites. Facilities: 3 restaurants, 5 bars, satellite TV, gym, Jacuzzi, windsurfing, scuba diving, sailing, snorkeling, 2 pools, disco, day-care center, boutique, 4 lighted tennis courts, volleyball, golf at Jamaica, Jamaica/Runaway Bay. AE, DC, MC, V. All-inclusive. Expensive.*

Chukka Cove. The battle cry at Chukka Cove is "Saddle Up." Chukka Cove earns its horse feed by maintaining some of the best equestrian facilities in the Western Hemisphere. In addition to polo, experienced riders will want to investigate Chukka Cove's Jamaican Riding Holiday, an exploration of the north coast on horseback. Less-dedicated riders have a choice of trail rides, mountain trail rides, beach rides, or an overnight escorted ride to the Lillyfield Great House. *Box 160, Ocho Rios, tel. 809/974-2593, fax 809/974-5568. 6 villas with 12 sets of private suites, with cook and maid. Facilities: stables, equestrian instruction (all levels), cooks to prepare meals in villas, swimming from rocks. No credit cards. EP, MAP, FAP. Expensive.*

The Enchanted Garden. Set on 20 acres in the former Carinosa Gardens, this all-inclusive resort opened its doors in the winter of 1991–1992. The gardens have been maintained and are stunning with tropical plants, flowers, and a dramatic series of streams and waterfalls. There is an aviary and a seaquarium where you can enjoy a delicatessen lunch or tea surrounded by tanks of fish and hanging orchids. The futuristic pink cinderblock villas regrettably seem incongruous amid the natural splendor, but the rooms are comfortable and you're never far from the soothing sound of rushing water. *Box 284, Ocho Rios, tel. 809/974-5346 or 800/323-5655, fax 809/974-5823. 112 villa suites, 40 with private plunge pool. Facilities: 4 restaurants, spa, disco, gift shop, beauty parlor, satellite TV, aviary, hillside gardens, 2 lighted tennis courts, and golf and horseback riding nearby. Daily transportation and picnic to private beach. AE, MC, V. All-inclusive. Expensive.*

Jamaica Grande. Ramada bought the Americana (Divi-Divi) and Mallards Beach resorts and created Jamaica Grande, now the largest conference hotel in Jamaica. A major refurbishment and the addition of a conference center were completed in mid-1993 at a cost of more than $20 million. This property attracts families, couples, conference attendees, and incentive-travel winners, who enjoy the focal point— the fantasy pool with waterfall, swaying bridge, and swim-up bar. Accommodations in the south building are a bit roomier, whereas those in the north boast slightly better views. The staff is quite friendly for such a large, and rather overwhelming, beachfront property. Families enjoy the daily Club Mongoose children's program. *Box 100, Ocho Rios, tel. 809/974–2201 or 800/228–9898, fax 809/974–5378. 691 rooms, 21 suites. Facilities: 5 restaurants, 8 bars, water-sports center, fitness center, disco, 4 tennis courts, daily supervised children's program, secretarial services, 3 pools, gaming parlor with slot machines, shopping arcade, beauty salon, 6 lighted tennis courts, 24-hr room service. AE, DC, MC, V. EP, MAP, All-inclusive. Expensive.*

★ **Sandals Dunn's River.** This luxury all-inclusive, couples-only resort in 23 acres of gardens opened its doors in winter 1991. A complete architectural reconstruction transformed the former Hilton/Eden II hotel into a Continental-Italian masterpiece. The accommodations are unusually spacious. This resort draws a well-heeled crowd in their thirties and forties and prides itself on catering to every guest's every whim. *Box 51, Ocho Rios, tel. 809/972–1610 or 800/SANDALS, fax 809/972–1611. 256 rooms. Facilities: 4 restaurants, beach, 2 swimming-pool bars, 3 whirlpools, water sports including scuba diving, 9-hole pitch-and-putt golf green, jogging course, 4 tennis courts (2 lighted), gaming parlor, disco, air-conditioned nightclub, satellite TV in all rooms. AE, MC, V. All-inclusive. Expensive.*

Sandals Ocho Rios. The Sandals concept follows its successful formula at this couples-only, all-inclusive, 9-acre beachfront resort. The mix of white and sand colors contrasts nicely with the vegetation and the sea. The accommodations are airy and pleasant, with king-size beds, air-conditioning, satellite TV, direct-dial phones, hair dryers, and safety deposit boxes. The resort is popular with honeymooners and more mature duos, with meandering paths through lush foliage, hammocks for two strung between trees, and cozy benches nestled amid flower beds for private stargazing. Activities include scuba diving, greens fees at, and transportation to, nearby Sandals Golf Club, and an excursion to Dunn's River Falls. *Ocho Rios, tel. 809/974–5691 or 800/SANDALS, fax 809/974–5700. 237* *units. Facilities: 3 restaurants, 4 bars, gift shop, 3 pools, 2 lighted tennis courts, disco, fitness center, satellite TV, water-sports center with scuba diving, golf nearby, tours. AE, DC, MC, V. All-inclusive. Expensive.*

Couples. No singles, no children. The emphasis at Couples is on romantic adventure for just the two of you, and the all-inclusive concept eliminates the decision making that can intrude on social pleasure. Couples has the highest occupancy rate of any resort on the island—and perhaps the most suggestive logo as well. There may be a correlation. *Tower Isle, St. Mary, tel. 809/975–4271 or 800/859–7873, fax 809/975–4439. 172 rooms, 12 suites. Facilities: 3 restaurants, 3 bars, 2 pools, satellite TV, island for nude swimming, 3 lighted tennis courts, Nautilus gym, 2 air-conditioned squash courts, a water-sports center that includes scuba diving, horseback riding, nightly entertainment, golf at Runaway Bay, 7 Jacuzzis, shopping arcade. AE, DC, MC, V. All-inclusive. Moderate–Expensive.*

Shaw Park Beach Hotel. Another popular property, Shaw Park offers a pleasant alternative to downtown high rises. All rooms have water views, air-conditioning, and telephones. The grounds are colorful and well tended, while the Silks disco is a favorite for late-night carousing. *Cutlass Bay, Box 17, Ocho Rios, tel. 809/974–2552 or 800/243–9420, fax 809/974–5042. 118 rooms. Facilities: restaurant, water sports, disco, pool, massage. AE, DC, MC, V. CP. Moderate.*

★ **Hibiscus Lodge.** This gleaming white building with a blue canopy sits amid beautifully manicured lawns laced with trellises, not too far from its tiny private beach. The impeccably neat, cozy rooms all have at least a partial sea view, terrace, air-conditioning, and full bath. This German-run property may be Jamaica's best bargain, attracting a discriminating (and jubilant) crowd. *Box 52, Ocho Rios, tel. 809/974–2676 or 800/JAMAICA, fax 809/974–1874. 26 rooms. Facilities: restaurant, pool, piano bar, lighted tennis court. AE, DC, MC, V. CP, MAP. Inexpensive.*

Jamel Continental. This spotless upscale tropical motel is set on its own beach in a relatively undeveloped area close to all the activities of Ocho Rios and Runaway Bay. The well-appointed units are spacious and breezy; all feature a balcony with sea view, full bath, phone, air-conditioning, and satellite TV. In addition to the usual floral prints and pastel hues, there are unexpected touches, such as mahogany writing desks and Oriental throw rugs. The moderately priced restaurant serves fine local dishes, and the staff is friendly and helpful. There's also a daily children's program, and the hotel is wheelchair-friendly. *2 Richmond Estate, Priory, St. Ann, tel. 809/972–1221, fax 809/972–0714. 21 rooms, 3 suites. Facilities: restaurant, bar, pool, Jacuzzi, gift shop. MC, V. MAP. Inexpensive.*

Port Antonio
★

Trident Villas and Hotel. If a single hotel had to be voted the most likely for coverage by "Lifestyles of the Rich and Famous," this would have to be it. Peacocks strut the manicured lawns; colonnaded walkways wind through whimsically sculpted topiary; and the pool, buried in a rocky bit of land jutting out into crashing surf, is a memory unto itself. The luxurious Laura Ashley–style rooms, many with turrets and bay windows, are awash in mahogany and lace. The truly gracious living will transport you back to the days of Empire. *Box 119, Port Antonio, tel. 809/993–2602 or 800/237–3237, fax 809/993–2590. 11 rooms, 16 suites. Facilities: restaurant, water sports, boutique, tennis court, pool. AE, MC, V. EP, MAP, FAP, All-inclusive. Very Expensive.*

Fern Hill Club. This is an all-inclusive hilltop property that's well run and usually full. The 16 new suites are bi-level and built into steep cliffs, with TVs, videos on request, small refrigerators, and a whirlpool-spa surrounded by a minigarden. The views are predictably spectacular. *Box 100, Port Antonio, tel. 809/993–3222 or 800/263–4354, fax 809/993–2257. 5 rooms, 16 suites, 5 1- and 2-bedroom apartments. Facilities: 3 pools, lighted tennis court, nightly entertainment, billiards, table tennis, shuffleboard, horseback riding (extra cost), transport to and from nearby San San beach, where scuba diving (extra cost) can be arranged. AE, MC, V. All-inclusive. Expensive.*

Goblin Hill. For a while this was known as the Jamaica Hill resort, but it is once again going by its original, evocative name. It's a lush 12-acre estate atop a hill overlooking San San cove. Each attractively appointed villa comes with its own dramatic view, plus a housekeeper-cook. Excellent villa and car-rental packages are available. *Box 26, Port Antonio, tel. 809/993–3286, fax 809/925–6248. 28 villas. Facilities: pool, beach, 2 tennis courts, water sports, reading and game room. AE, MC, V. EP. Expensive.*

Jamaica Palace. Errol Flynn might have loved this place for its sense of style and humor. Built to resemble an Edwardian mansion, this imposing five-year-old property rises in an expanse of white pillared marble, with the all-white theme continued on the interior, broken only by the black lacquer and gilded oversize furniture. Each room has a semicircular bed and original European objets d'art and Oriental rugs; some are more lavish than others. Although the hotel is not on the beach, there is a 114-foot swimming pool shaped like Jamaica. *Box 227, Port Antonio, tel. 809/993–2021 or 800/423–4095, fax 809/993–3459. 54 rooms, 5 suites, 20 junior suites. Facilities: restaurant, 2 bars, pool, baby-sitters on request, boutique. AE, MC, V. EP, MAP. Moderate.*

Bonnie View Plantation Hotel. Though the main appeal of this property is to the budget, it does have a few nice rooms with private verandas overlooking spectacular scenery. Its restaurant atop a 600-foot hill offers the finest view of all. *Box 82, Port Antonio, tel. 809/993–2752 or 800/423–4095, fax 809/993–2862. 20 rooms. Facilities: restaurant, pool, sun deck. AE, DC, MC, V. EP. Inexpensive.*

DeMontevin Lodge. This historic place offers the ambience of a more genteel time. The rooms are basic and spotless, with circular fans overhead. Outsiders are welcome for very tasty home-cooking at lunch or dinner, with prior reservations. *Fort George St. on Titchfield Hill, Port Antonio, tel. 809/993–2604. 15 rooms. Facilities: restaurant, bar. AE. EP. Inexpensive.*

Runaway Bay

★ **FDR, Franklyn D. Resort.** Jamaica's first all-suite, all-inclusive resort for families, this fabulous answer to parents' prayers opened in 1990. Upscale yet unpretentious, the pink buildings house spacious and well-thought-out one-, two-, and three-bedroom villas and are grouped in a horseshoe around the swimming pool. Best of all, a "girl Friday" comes with each suite, filling the role of nanny, housekeeper, and (when desired) cook. She'll even baby-sit at night for a small charge. Most parents are so impressed that they wish they could take their girl Friday home with them when they leave. Children and teens are kept busy with day-long supervised activities and sports, while parents are free to join in, lounge around the pool, play golf, go scuba diving, or just enjoy uninterrupted time together getting reacquainted. *Runaway Bay, tel. 809/973–3067 or 800/654–1FDR, fax 809/973–3071. 67 suites. Facilities: restaurant, pool, water sports including scuba diving, beach, gym, satellite TV, lighted tennis court, golf, disco, piano bar, miniclub for children with supervised activities, petting zoo, piano bar, beach across the street, glass-bottom-boat tour. AE, MC, V. All-inclusive. Expensive–Very Expensive.*

Jamaica, Jamaica. This all-inclusive was a pioneer in emphasizing the sheer Jamaican-ness of the island. The cooking is particularly first-rate, with an emphasis on Jamaican cuisine and fresh seafood. Lodgings are rather spartan, resembling tropical dorm rooms, but comfortable, with amenities that include hair dryers and safety deposit boxes. The happy campers don't mind; Germans, Italians, and Japanese flock here for the psychedelically colored reef surrounding the beach and the superb golf school (plans are afoot to make the already excellent course more challenging). Those seeking more upscale accommodations should request the beachfront one-bedroom suites, which were renovated in 1993. *Box 58, Runaway Bay, tel. 809/973–2436 or 800/859–7873, fax 809/973–2352. 238 rooms, 4 suites. Facilities: 2 restaurants, 2 bars, water-sports center, 2 lighted tennis courts, horseback riding, PADI 5-star dive* *center, gym, sundry shop, sightseeing tours, disco, nightly entertainment, 3 Jacuzzis, 18-hole golf course with golf school nearby. Guests must be over 16. AE, DC, MC, V. All-inclusive. Expensive.*

Club Caribbean. This resort reopened its doors in winter 1990 after a $3 million renovation and became all-inclusive in 1992, catering to families on a budget. A series of 128 typically Caribbean cottages, 68 with kitchenette, lines the long but narrow beach. The rooms are simple but clean, with rattan furnishings and floral prints. Very popular with European families (children under 7 stay free, and 60 cottages feature bunk beds instead of kitchenettes). While most water sports are included, scuba diving costs extra. *Box 65, Runaway Bay, tel. 809/973–3507 or 800/ 223–9815, fax 809/973–3509. 128 rooms. Facilities: 2 restaurants, pool, shopping arcade, PADI 5-star dive center, water-sports center, 2 tennis courts, massage and exercise, day-care center with children's program. AE, MC, V. All-inclusive. Inexpensive.*

H.E.A.R.T. Country Club. It's a shame more visitors don't know about this place, perched above Runaway Bay and brimming with Jamaica's true character. While training young islanders interested in the tourism industry— H.E.A.R.T. stands for Human Employment And Resource Training—it also provides a remarkably quiet and pleasant stay for guests. The employees make an effort to please. Accommodations have air-conditioning and private baths and either an ocean or garden view. The tranquil restaurant serves delicious local and Continental specialties. *Box 98, St. Ann, tel. 809/973–2671 or 800/JAMAICA, fax 809/973– 2693. 20 rooms. Facilities: restaurant, satellite TV, golf, beach shuttle. AE, MC, V. EP, All–inclusive. Inexpensive.*

8 The Arts and Nightlife

Jamaica—especially Kingston—supports a lively community of musicians. For starters there is reggae, popularized by the late Bob Marley and the Wailers and performed today by son Ziggy Marley, Jimmy Tosh (the late Peter Tosh's son), Gregory Isaacs, the Third World, Jimmy Cliff, and many others. If your experience of Caribbean music has been limited to steel drums and Harry Belafonte, then the political, racial, and religious messages of reggae may set you on your ear; listen closely and you just might hear the heartbeat of the people. Those who already love reggae may want to plan a visit in mid-July to August for the Reggae Sunsplash. The four-night concert at the Bob Marley Performing Center (a field set up with a temporary stage), in the Freeport area of Montego Bay, showcases local talent and attracts such performers as Rick James, Gladys Knight and the Pips, Steel Pulse, Third World, and Ziggy Marley and the Melody Makers.

Discos and Clubs

For the most part, the liveliest late-night happenings throughout Jamaica are in the major resort hotels. Some of the best music will be found in Negril at **De Buss** (tel. 809/957–4405) and of course at the hot, hot spot, **Kaiser's Cafe** (tel. 809/957–4070), as well as at the **disco** at Hedonism II (tel. 809/957–4200), and **Compulsion Disco** (tel. 809/957–4416). The most popular spots in Kingston are **Godfather** (Knutsford Blvd., tel. 809/929–5459), **Mingles** at the Courtleigh (tel. 809/929–5321), **Illusions** in the New Lane Plaza (tel. 809/929–2125), and **Jonkanoo** in the Wyndham New Kingston (tel. 809/929–3390).

In Port Antonio, if you have but one night to disco, do it at the **Roof Club**, 11 West Street (no phone). On weekends, from eleven-ish on, this is where it's all happening. If you want to "do the town," check out **CenterPoint** on Folly Road (tel. 809/993–3377), **Shadows** at 40 West Street (tel. 809/993–3823), or the Jamaican cultural show on Friday nights at **Fern Hill Club** (tel. 809/993–3222). The principal clubs in Ocho Rios are **Acropolis** at 70 Main Street (tel. 809/974–2633), **Silks** in the Shaw Park Beach Hotel (tel. 809/

974–2552), and the **Little Pub on Main Street** (tel. 809/974–2324), which produces Caribbean revues. The hottest places in Montego Bay are the **Cave** disco at the Seawinds Beach Resort (tel. 809/952–4070), **Sir Winston's Reggae Club** on Gloucester Street (tel. 809/952–2084), and the **Rhythm Nightclub** at the Holiday Inn (tel. 809/953–2485). After 10 PM on Friday nights, the crowd gathers at **Pier 1** on Howard Cooke Blvd., opposite the straw market (tel. 809/952–2452). Some of the all-inclusives offer a dinner and disco pass from about $50.

Index

Personal Itinerary

Departure *Date*

Time

Transportation

Arrival *Date*   *Time*

Departure *Date*   *Time*

Transportation

Arrival *Date*   *Time*

Departure *Date*   *Time*

Transportation

Arrival *Date*   *Time*

Departure *Date*   *Time*

Transportation

Personal Itinerary

Arrival *Date*   *Time*

Departure *Date*   *Time*

Transportation

Arrival *Date*   *Time*

Departure *Date*   *Time*

Transportation

Arrival *Date*   *Time*

Departure *Date*   *Time*

Transportation

Arrival *Date*   *Time*

Departure *Date*   *Time*

Transportation

Personal Itinerary

Arrival *Date*   *Time*

Departure *Date*   *Time*

Transportation

Arrival *Date*   *Time*

Departure *Date*   *Time*

Transportation

Arrival *Date*   *Time*

Departure *Date*   *Time*

Transportation

Arrival *Date*   *Time*

Departure *Date*   *Time*

Transportation

Personal Itinerary

Arrival	*Date*	*Time*
Departure	*Date*	*Time*
Transportation		

Arrival	*Date*	*Time*
Departure	*Date*	*Time*
Transportation		

Arrival	*Date*	*Time*
Departure	*Date*	*Time*
Transportation		

Arrival	*Date*	*Time*
Departure	*Date*	*Time*
Transportation		

Addresses

Name	*Name*
Address	*Address*
Telephone	*Telephone*
Name	*Name*
Address	*Address*
Telephone	*Telephone*
Name	*Name*
Address	*Address*
Telephone	*Telephone*
Name	*Name*
Address	*Address*
Telephone	*Telephone*
Name	*Name*
Address	*Address*
Telephone	*Telephone*
Name	*Name*
Address	*Address*
Telephone	*Telephone*
Name	*Name*
Address	*Address*
Telephone	*Telephone*
Name	*Name*
Address	*Address*
Telephone	*Telephone*

Addresses

Name	*Name*
Address	*Address*
Telephone	*Telephone*
Name	*Name*
Address	*Address*
Telephone	*Telephone*
Name	*Name*
Address	*Address*
Telephone	*Telephone*
Name	*Name*
Address	*Address*
Telephone	*Telephone*
Name	*Name*
Address	*Address*
Telephone	*Telephone*
Name	*Name*
Address	*Address*
Telephone	*Telephone*
Name	*Name*
Address	*Address*
Telephone	*Telephone*
Name	*Name*
Address	*Address*
Telephone	*Telephone*

The only guide to explore a Disney World® you've never seen before:
The one for grown-ups.

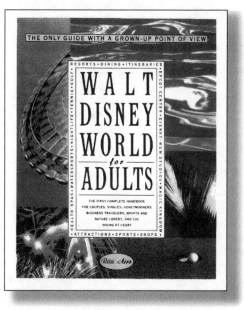

0-679-02490-5 $14.00 ($18.50 Can)

This is the only guide written specifically for the millions of adults who visit Walt Disney World® each year <u>without</u> kids. Upscale, sophisticated, packed full of facts and maps, *Walt Disney World® for Adults* provides up-to-date information on hotels, restaurants, sports facilities, and health clubs, as well as unique itineraries for adults. With *Walt Disney World® for Adults* in hand, readers get the most out of one of the world's most fascinating, most complex playgrounds.

At bookstores everywhere, or call **1-800-533-6478**.

Fodor's Travel Guides

Available at bookstores everywhere, or call 1–800–533–6478, 24 hours a day.

U.S. Guides

Alaska

Arizona

Boston

California

Cape Cod, Martha's Vineyard, Nantucket

The Carolinas & the Georgia Coast

Chicago

Colorado

Florida

Hawaii

Las Vegas, Reno, Tahoe

Los Angeles

Maine, Vermont, New Hampshire

Maui

Miami & the Keys

New England

New Orleans

New York City

Pacific North Coast

Philadelphia & the Pennsylvania Dutch Country

The Rockies

San Diego

San Francisco

Santa Fe, Taos, Albuquerque

Seattle & Vancouver

The South

The U.S. & British Virgin Islands

USA

The Upper Great Lakes Region

Virginia & Maryland

Waikiki

Walt Disney World and the Orlando Area

Washington, D.C.

Foreign Guides

Acapulco, Ixtapa, Zihuatanejo

Australia & New Zealand

Austria

The Bahamas

Baja & Mexico's Pacific Coast Resorts

Barbados

Berlin

Bermuda

Brittany & Normandy

Budapest

Canada

Cancún, Cozumel, Yucatán Peninsula

Caribbean

China

Costa Rica, Belize, Guatemala

The Czech Republic & Slovakia

Eastern Europe

Egypt

Euro Disney

Europe

Florence, Tuscany & Umbria

France

Germany

Great Britain

Greece

Hong Kong

India

Ireland

Israel

Italy

Japan

Kenya & Tanzania

Korea

London

Madrid & Barcelona

Mexico

Montréal & Québec City

Morocco

Moscow & St. Petersburg

The Netherlands, Belgium & Luxembourg

New Zealand

Norway

Nova Scotia, Prince Edward Island & New Brunswick

Paris

Portugal

Provence & the Riviera

Rome

Russia & the Baltic Countries

Scandinavia

Scotland

Singapore

South America

Southeast Asia

Spain

Sweden

Switzerland

Thailand

Tokyo

Toronto

Turkey

Vienna & the Danube Valley

Special Series

Fodor's Affordables
Caribbean
Europe
Florida
France
Germany
Great Britain
Italy
London
Paris

Fodor's Bed & Breakfast and Country Inns Guides
America's Best B&Bs
California
Canada's Great Country Inns
Cottages, B&Bs and Country Inns of England and Wales
Mid-Atlantic Region
New England
The Pacific Northwest
The South
The Southwest
The Upper Great Lakes Region

The Berkeley Guides
California
Central America
Eastern Europe
Europe
France
Germany & Austria
Great Britain & Ireland
Italy
London

Mexico
Pacific Northwest & Alaska
Paris
San Francisco

Fodor's Exploring Guides
Australia
Boston & New England
Britain
California
The Caribbean
Florence & Tuscany
Florida
France
Germany
Ireland
Italy
London
Mexico
New York City
Paris
Prague
Rome
Scotland
Singapore & Malaysia
Spain
Thailand
Turkey

Fodor's Flashmaps
Boston
New York
Washington, D.C.

Fodor's Pocket Guides
Acapulco
Bahamas

Barbados
Jamaica
London
New York City
Paris
Puerto Rico
San Francisco
Washington, D.C.

Fodor's Sports
Cycling
Golf Digest's Best Places to Play
Hiking
The Insider's Guide to the Best Canadian Skiing
Running
Sailing
Skiing in the USA & Canada
USA Today's Complete Four Sports Stadium Guide

Fodor's Three-In-Ones (guidebook, language cassette, and phrase book)
France
Germany
Italy
Mexico
Spain

Fodor's Special-Interest Guides
Complete Guide to America's National Parks
Condé Nast Traveler Caribbean Resort and Cruise Ship Finder

Cruises and Ports of Call
Euro Disney
France by Train
Halliday's New England Food Explorer
Healthy Escapes
Italy by Train
London Companion
Shadow Traffic's New York Shortcuts and Traffic Tips
Sunday in New York
Sunday in San Francisco
Touring Europe
Touring USA: Eastern Edition
Walt Disney World and the Orlando Area
Walt Disney World for Adults

Fodor's Vacation Planners
Great American Learning Vacations
Great American Sports & Adventure Vacations
Great American Vacations
Great American Vacations for Travelers with Disabilities
National Parks and Seashores of the East
National Parks of the West

The Wall Street Journal Guides to Business Travel

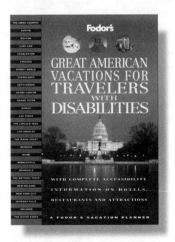